THEME
AND
STRATEGY

ABOUT THE AUTHOR

Ronald Tobias has spent his career as a writer moving from genre to genre, first as a short story writer, then as an author of fiction and nonfiction books, and finally as a writer and producer of documentaries for public television. He is a Professor in the Department of Media and Theatre Arts at Montana State University. Among his nonfiction books are *Our Man Is Inside* and *Shoot to Kill*; his fiction includes *Kings and Desperate Men and Other Stories* and *The Bodywasher*.

THEME
AND
STRATEGY

BY

RONALD TOBIAS

CINCINNATI, OHIO

Theme and Strategy. Copyright © 1989 by Ronald Tobias. Printed and bound in the United States of America. All rights reserved. No part of this book may be reproduced in any form or by any electronic or mechanical means including information storage and retrieval systems without permission in writing from the publisher, except by a reviewer, who may quote brief passages in a review. Published by Writer's Digest Books, an imprint of F&W Publications, Inc., 1507 Dana Ave., Cincinnati, Ohio 45207. First edition.

93 92 91 90 89   5 4 3 2 1

Library of Congress Cataloging-in-Publication Data

Tobias, Ron.
  Theme and strategy / Ronald Tobias.
    p. cm.
  ISBN 0-89879-392-0
  1. Authorship. I. Title.
PN151.T6 1989
  808.3 — dc20   89-39363
                                   CIP

To Valerie, Always

CONTENTS

CHAPTER 1

PATTERN IN STRATEGY

LEARNING TO WIN:
THE IMPORTANCE OF STRATEGY

A battle fought without strategy is nearly always lost. Whether that battle is fought on a muddy field in Europe or on a chessboard in the park or in an uptown corporate office makes no difference: success rarely belongs to those who seek it blindly. The doctor who decides the best way to treat a patient, the lawyer who decides the best defense for a client, and the businessman who decides the best way to sell a product all depend upon deciding and pursuing a course of action that will give them the best chance to reach their goal successfully. No professional sports team dare take the field without a strategy, no politician dare campaign without one, and no author should write without one. The stakes are too high and the investment is too great to entrust success to chance.

Strategy Is Both Map and Journey

About this time you have an idea for a story in mind. You know what you want to write, but you're not sure *how* to write it. You have two choices: either bulldoze your way ahead and trust the gods will take care of you, or develop a strategy to guide you through the work. The choice is yours, eyes open or closed.

Obviously, if you choose to trust luck, then you don't need this book or any book to help you; but if you agree with me that writing is also planning, and good planning makes good writing, then you'll want to learn how to create sound strategy.

Strategy is a unified course of action that guides your decisions about what choices to make as a writer. The other books in this series have concentrated on individual techniques — plot, character, dialogue, and so forth — but this book addresses a more important issue: how to make the different techniques work together effectively. Knowing how to write crackling action or convincing dialogue may make good writing, but these things in themselves don't make good fiction. Writing is more than flour and water and eggs carelessly tossed together in a bowl; you have to know what proportions are appropriate, too. How much characterization should you develop for the kind of plot you've chosen? How much action is too much? Too little? Strategy becomes your recipe for writing — the guide that you follow to get the right mix of plot, character, action, and theme.

The success of a work of fiction depends upon more than just the variety of good techniques: it depends upon your ability to create relationships between your characters and your action, between plot and theme, and each of the major elements of fiction, so that all the parts of the whole work together for a single purpose. Without strategy, your effort will have no direction and no purpose, no matter how brilliantly you master technique. Without strategy, trying to write would be like going duck hunting with a blindfold on. Your quarry will keep flying right by you.

The secret in writing isn't in simply knowing what ingredients go into its making, but in knowing how to make those ingredients work together.

This book looks at the elements of fiction as a connected whole rather than a bunch of disconnected parts. It will show you how the techniques of fiction relate to each other, and more importantly, it will show you how to tailor a strategy that works for you and for your work. It will answer such questions as how to make character and plot work together for the best effect; how to tackle such formidable concepts as pattern, theme, and symbolism.

ON YOUR MARK

Don't think of writing as a blind sprint to the finish line. Writing is like long-distance running. Think of the short story as a one-mile run, the screenplay and the novella as a ten-kilometer run, and the novel, which requires the greatest endurance of all, as a marathon. Writing requires stamina, strength, and perhaps more importantly, it requires strategy. The experienced runner knows the race usually doesn't go to the fleetest of foot: it goes to the person who knows best how to run the course. As conditions change, the smart runner alters his strategy to fit those conditions. The wind may change and speed him up or slow him down; he may get boxed in by other runners; or perhaps he develops a cramp in his leg. He has to rethink, recalculate, and then refigure. He's like a computer that constantly makes changes according to new input. The goal remains the same — to reach the finish line before everyone else — but the method to reach that goal constantly gets readjusted. So it is with writing. The unexpected always happens. A sound strategy will help prepare you to deal with the unexpected and to avoid some of the pitfalls.

The concept of strategy may sound ominous to you at first. Your reaction may be, "I've already got my hands full worrying about plot and character. I don't have time to worry about *strategy*. The truth is you can't afford *not* to worry about strategy. In all the years I've been teaching writing workshops, and after reading literally thousands of stories and hundreds of screenplays and novels by aspiring writers, it's easy for me to tell which writers are taking a shot in the dark and which are working within the framework of a strategy. The writer who hopes that strategy will somehow take care of itself (trusting it to that slippery catch-all hope we call *intuition*) is like a person who runs with his eyes closed. Sooner or later (and probably sooner) he's going to run off-track and into disaster. As a writer, the farther you wander off the track, the less likely you will be to find your way back. Too many stories with good ideas fail to keep their promise only because the writer didn't have a proper guidance system. Too many wonderful characters get buried and too many brilliant plots spoiled because the writer either didn't know how to formulate a strategy or how to follow it. These failures happen because writers rely too frequently on dumb luck. Sometimes we call it faith: the belief that everything in our work will turn out as it should. Instead of taking responsibility for the direction of our work, we take the attitude that there's no point in trying to control what we've been told a thousand times can't be controlled. How many times have you heard someone say you can't control creativity, so just lie back and let it happen?

Don't believe it.

True, we think of writing as a mystical act. Because of this, creativity is paradoxical. The harder you try to be creative, the harder it is to be creative. Psychologists tell us that creativity happens only when we can relax the conscious mind enough for the unconscious mind to express itself. Nobody can always be creative on demand. But during those moments when we're lucky enough to be creative, we need to be ready as much as possible to channel that energy into a productive direction rather than let it spill out helter-skelter.

You need to shape your creative output as it emerges. And this is my point. Without a strategy to guide and shape your creativity, then you give up any control of it. Don't just throw the deck of cards up into the air and hope that fate will deal you a good hand. If you have a good idea for a work, do what you can to give your idea a chance not only to survive but to flourish.

Footsteps

The actual record of a race is contained in the footsteps them-selves, just as the record of a work of fiction is contained in the words. The race is comprised of footsteps, and each footstep constitutes a decision made by the runner about where he wants to be on the track. Every word you write also constitutes a decision made by you about where you want to be. Every step you take, every word you write is part of a pattern, and *pattern* is the real backbone of fiction.

You've probably heard the argument that *plot* is the backbone of fiction or that *character* is. True, these elements and others are critical to the success of your work, but their success depends in large part on the patterns you create for them, and how those patterns integrate with the other major patterns of your work. Pattern is deep structure.

Deep structure is different from dramatic structure, which concerns itself with rising and falling action, climax, and denouement. Deep structure permeates every molecule of your writing. It reflects not only in the obvious elements of plot and character but also in subtler — but no less important — elements such as style, imagery, symbolism, and tone. *Deep structure* is the glue that holds the work together and unifies its constituent parts. *Pattern* creates the weave that holds together the fabric of your story, and *strategy* is the action that you take as a writer to accomplish sound and meaningful patterns in what you write.

The common denominator among the sciences, the arts, and the humanities is pattern. The aim of physics, for example, is to discover the pattern of events that control the natural world: Why do planets move the way they do? What rules govern atoms? The aim of biology is to discover the pattern of nature: Why do lemmings run into the sea? Why do birds migrate? The aim of psychology is to discover the patterns of human and animal behavior: why do animals act as they do? Mathematics is pure pattern. So is music, dance, architecture, and, of course, literature.

The difference between physics (or any of the sciences) and fiction, however, is that in fiction the writer actually constructs the design whereas in physics the task is only to discover the pattern and interpret it. In this sense you have a broader responsibility as a writer. You have the freedom to create any world you want, but you also must make sure that the internal and external organization of that world is consistent. That fearsome task is accomplished by the use of strategy.

Anyone who's taken the time to marvel at the intricacies of nature can't help but be impressed by its deep structure. Even seemingly trivial details, such as the coloration of a moth or the shape of a flower petal, are links in an ecological chain that unifies all living things. Wherever you look in nature you find the same major themes repeated, the same major patterns expressed, the same application of thinking throughout the system of life. Despite the titanic complexity of nature, it is one elegant, unified pattern — the ecosystem of life.

Good fiction strives to achieve the same goal. The appearance of what may seem like trivial details (of conversation or of description, for example) are in fact meaningful elements of a carefully constructed pattern. The writer creates a set of laws for the fiction to which everything must ultimately conform.

Sometimes you hear the claim that the writer is a god, free to create worlds at will. What you don't often hear, however, is that with the power to create other worlds also comes the burden of responsibility to make those worlds work. We are never truly free as writers, despite our powers of creation, because we are held accountable (by our readers) to make only wholly logical worlds in which every detail fits snugly into an overall scheme of things. An awesome responsibility, but one that can be accomplished with careful forethought.

Throughout the centuries of civilization, we've dedicated ourselves to the pursuit of discovering and discerning the meaning of patterns. When the ancients stared at the thousands of stars in the heavens at night, they rejected randomness in favor of order and discovered (or invented) patterns that became our present-day constellations — the Great Bear, the Swan, the Eagle, and hundreds of others. Our ancestors divined meaning in the patterns of the liver and stomachs of animals, in the geometry of bones, in the lines in the palm of a hand or the bumps on a skull, or in the progression of tarot cards laid upon a table. In patterns we attempt to discover meaning that allows us to try to tackle the greater problem of existence. Patterns are fundamental to human nature. We like to create them (the arts) and we like to discover them (the sciences). In writing, these two powerful forces combine: as artists we create the patterns, but we create them for our audiences to find.

Don't underestimate the power of this bond between you, as the creator of a work, and your audience. A story works because it creates a sense of expectation about what's going to happen next or why something happened the way it did. Recently I was riding a chairlift at a ski area and I saw a skier ahead and below me inching out onto a ledge that had a straight drop of about thirty feet below it. I could see, but the skier couldn't, that he was creeping beyond the rock shelf and onto nothing but snow. Would the snow hold him up? Would he pull back in time? In the half-second these questions raced through my head, the snow cushion gave way under the skier and I watched as he plummeted off the ledge and into a pine tree below him. I was powerless. Was he hurt? He fell out of my line of sight and I couldn't tell what happened to him. Fortunately I was only seconds away from the top of the lift, and I told the lift attendant, who immediately sent out the ski patrol.

The experience I went through watching and not knowing what had happened to that skier kept me thinking all afternoon. Seeing him balanced precariously on that ledge, and knowing that the ledge could give way, created within me the anticipation of disaster. And seeing him fall and not knowing if he was hurt or not had done the same. One was a short-term expectation and the other was long-term, which built up the drama of the event. I recognized the pattern of carelessness (on the part of the skier, who should have known better) and the ingredients of potential disaster. Then reality made me wait (thus increasing the tension) to find out the outcome, just as I am doing now to you.

The skier, it turned out, had bruised his ego more than his body. But the image of him catapulted off that ledge and into that pine tree and then falling through the branches is indelible. I still don't know how he escaped serious injury. I do know, however, the effects of the event on me, the observer — effects that were the result of interpreting the patterns of plot, character, and action. Pattern allows the reader to *participate* in your work in the same way that I, as a witness, participated in the skier's disaster.

The twentieth-century philosopher Alfred North Whitehead perhaps gave the clearest definition of art when he described it as *pattern imposed upon experience*. Think for a moment what that means, because it explains a major difference between art and reality. Reality is raw experience. Life is tumultuous, chaotic at times, and filled with chance and coincidence, while fiction is orderly, not random, and hates chance and coincidence. The world inside a work of fiction is highly ordered and logical, whereas in our lives we rarely can explain why things happen the way they do. But while our world is open-ended, the world inside a work of fiction is always close-ended. Fiction, unlike life, has clear beginnings, middles, and ends. Its world is very precise and accountable. There is a reason for everything that happens. In short, nothing happens that shouldn't happen.

The necessity for logic is the foundation for pattern. When, for example, events progress according to some rational method, then they automatically create a pattern that we call cause and effect: Michael meets Mary; they fall in love; they marry and live happily ever after. When a character behaves consistently with his personality, then his actions will automatically create a pattern. And so it is with each technique, from plot to style. What would a reader think if you wrote the first fifty pages of your work in the style of Judith Krantz and the next fifty pages in the style of James Joyce, for no reason? If you violate the many patterns in your work, then you risk jolting the reader out of the world you've created and breaking the illusion of the fiction. When you hear someone say, "He'd never do that," or "That would never happen," what that person is really saying is: You've disturbed the fiction by violating the patterns of character and plot. And when you violate the patterns within your work, then you lock out the reader.

Since art is pattern imposed upon experience, that means you have to take all your raw material (either from life or from your imagination) and shape it. Don't make the mistake of thinking that writing is simply an act of recording the details of what goes on in life. Fiction likes to masquerade as reality. Ironically, even though fiction is an illusion, we still manage to find reality in it.

Shaping your fiction means developing a strategy. It means answering such hard questions as "What do I want to say?" and "How do I want to say it?" If your goal is simply to write an entertaining work without a real "message," or if you intend to write a serious work, you'll have to come to terms with these questions at some point, and the sooner you do the easier it will be for you to write the work you hoped to write.

GET SET

Some writers know from the start exactly what they want to do and how they want to do it. Other writers have a general idea or at least a vague concept of what they want to do. A third group of writers have no idea at all how they intend to write their story.

The first group of writers won't begin a work unless they know precisely what should happen to whom, when, where, and why. They have notebooks filled with data detailing everything down to the social security numbers of the characters. The second group has jotted down some notes here and there, on scraps of paper or on index cards or in a journal. Instead of painstaking portraits, their characters start out looking more like stick figures drawn by a first-grader. The third group of writers pretty much fly into a work on a wing and a prayer. No real plans, no real ideas, just an urge to write. Which of the three groups do you belong to?

Let's take the first group: people who have a complete set of blueprints before they begin construction. Before they write page one, they can tell you in exquisite detail what the story is, who the story is about, what the plot and subplots are, what the major themes are, and on and on. They're so involved in the work that they've done everything possible except write it. If you've ever listened to a writer in this first group go into detail about his or her work, you couldn't help but be impressed and maybe even a touch jealous.

So, you ask, what's wrong with that?

Too much strategy can stifle a work just as easily as no strategy. Blueprints are wonderful things for building houses. But a blueprint is the architect's *final draft*. All the creative thinking has already been finished. An outline for a work of fiction *isn't* a final draft; it isn't even a first draft! It's a *preconception*.

The danger lies in treating a preconception like an architect's blueprint. Some writers know, as Robert Burns said, "The best laid schemes o' mice and men/ Gang aft a-gley." There is always something to upset the most careful of human calculations. Once you begin the actual writing, it is inevitable as day follows night that the writing will "stray" from even the most careful blueprint. A character will suddenly do or say something that's completely out of the plan. What should you do if this happens? Should you go back and make the character do and say what you originally intended for him? Or should you go ahead and let the character do and say what he or she wants?

Remember my analogy of the runner? The writer who insists on making happen what he believes should happen according to a preconception is like a runner who removes himself mentally from the race by sticking inflexibly to a game plan. The difference is between the runner's belief about how the race should be run versus how the race is actually being run. He willfully blinds himself to the event rather than adapt to it. He ignores the fallen runner who was pacing the race; he pushes himself harder if he can't keep the pace, even if there is a head wind slowing him (and everyone else) down. And unless you can predict the future perfectly, the plan and the event are rarely ever the same.

Conditions on the track change all the time. Unexpected opportunities arise, and good writers, like good runners, learn to capitalize on the unexpected. Sometimes running slower is faster; and if the shortest distance between two points is a straight line, it may not be the fastest route, and so a runner with a sharp eye looks for the advantage that suddenly and unexpectedly presents itself.

As a writer you need to design an overall strategy that allows you to be open-minded enough to allow the hidden to emerge on its own, unhampered by your ideas of what *ought* to happen. Don't lock yourself into a single mindset. Trust your creative input; don't reject something just because it doesn't conform to your original idea about the work. More often than not, the wiser decision is to go with your characters and do what they want to do rather than what you want them to do. Somehow they know themselves better than you do.

Pretend for a moment that you're a character in a story written by an obsessive writer. It's your first day on vacation in New York. You consult the itinerary the author has laid out for you:

5:25, wake up

5:30-5:45, shower

5:45-6:00, dress (wear the cotton small floral print skirt with the shell-pink cotton-knit sweater from Villager and the Cole-Haan white leather moccasins)

6:00-6:05, take the elevator downstairs

6:05-6:45, eat breakfast (one egg, boiled five minutes, dry toast, coffee, a small glass of tomato juice)

and so on minute by minute throughout the day for each day of your vacation. If you're at all like me, you'd be screaming after you saw the wake-up time. No way, you say. This is a *vacation*. I do what I want to do, when I want to do it. It's okay to have an itinerary for your characters, but they demand a certain amount of freedom to make their own choices. Don't stifle them with obsessive planning. Treat your characters as you would want the author to treat you if you were a character. Planning is good — up to a point.

Now let's take the other extreme — people who have no idea about the structure of the work or what their characters should do and when they should do it. Just as the first group were overguided, so this group is underguided. Rather than having too much direction, these people have absolutely no direction and so most of their energy goes into trying to find out what they're doing and where they're headed.

Creativity is fluid and, like water, it is formless and always conforms to the container that holds it. If there's no vessel to contain the water, then it will run off and drain endlessly. Such is the danger of having too little or no preconception of the story you want to write.

This type of writer has an awful time developing any sort of momentum because he has to spend most of his energy trying to figure out what the work is and what to do with it. He has no framework to think within, no vessel to shape his free-flowing creativity. Not until he develops a strategy can he move forward.

A rusty argument surfaces from time to time that disputes this idea of having a strategy to guide your creativity. The argument insists that a 'blank' mind lets a work emerge from your mind in its purest form. Look how Mozart wrote entire musical scores in a single sitting, how Edgar Allan Poe wrote his most famous poem, "The Raven," in an afternoon, and how Samuel Taylor Coleridge's most famous poem, "Xanadu," ("In Xanadu did Kubla Khan,/ a stately pleasure dome decree . . .") came to him word for word in a dream. There are dozens, perhaps hundreds of other examples like these.

Time to debunk these pesky myths. We like to believe that true genius is unexpected and instantaneous. We like to believe that the world's greatest operas, symphonies, novels, and poems flow effortlessly out of the pens of geniuses. This ability to create instantaneously and without need of revision adds to the mystique of the artist, who's considered truly inspired—chosen by the gods as it were—to bring art to man.

All very romantic, but it's bunk.

Actually it's a throwback to the days of the Greeks and Romans who believed that the gods actually breathed art into select men (and never women). Hence the word *inspire*, which means to breathe into. But, according to modern psychology, inspiration doesn't come from such outside sources as the stars or the gods, but from the inside, from the unconscious mind.

The unconscious mind, while capable of amazing feats, isn't capable of making something out of nothing. The truth about our geniuses is that many of them lied outright about their amazing feats. Many writers liked to give the false impression that they "dashed off" their great works when in fact they slaved over them. Edgar Allan Poe didn't write "The Raven" in an afternoon; the poem took him *three years*, and even then he probably stole the famous refrain "Nevermore" from another poem of the time. Samuel Taylor Coleridge, who claimed to have written "Xanadu" completely from a dream, was also misrepresenting the truth. His "dream," as he called it, was more of a hallucination as the result of smoking opium, and although he did write a draft of the poem, historical evidence proves that the idea had already occurred to Coleridge at least *two years* before he actually wrote it. And so it goes, as biographers document the facts that many writers either misrepresent, distort, or intentionally lie about how "easy" it was to create their masterpieces.

Of course not all writers are so underhanded. Some actually do sit down and write from beginning to end without stopping. But again the evidence shows that even in such cases where the writer seems to have been divinely inspired, the idea had been "rattling around" inside his or her head for months or even years, so that when the time came to commit pen to paper, the material had already organized itself subconsciously.

The important point to remember is that every writer needs a framework to think within. If the framework is too rigid, then you cut off any possibility for creative development. If the framework is either too shapeless or nonexistent, then your creativity will have a hard time building momentum. The best state for a writer to be in is to have a structure that is flexible enough to allow the work to develop according to its needs, but not so flexible that it rambles from page to page in a desperate search for structure or meaning.

GO!

How do you accomplish this delicate balance between conscious structure and unconscious content?

There is no easy answer to this question. Strategy is as much an attitude as it is a plan. But there are some basic guidelines you can follow that will help.

First, pick two points in the story:

1. *Start with a beginning*. Notice I didn't say start *in* the beginning. The beginning isn't just the first page you write; it's your sense of where the *story* should start, and,

2. *Pick an ending*. The ending is nothing more than your sense of how the story might end. Writing the story becomes a matter of connecting the two points: beginning and end. It may very well be that your beginning ends up in the middle, and that your end ends up being not part of the work at all. But that's

not the issue. You've given yourself a place to start and you've pointed yourself in a direction. You've taken the first step toward developing a strategy: determining a specific goal.

3. *Set short-term objectives.* The end is a long-term objective. Strategy, however, is composed of both a long-term objective and several short-term objectives. The short-term objectives are the individual dramatic units of your work, whether they be scenes, the sequences of a screenplay, acts, or chapters. Dramatic structure is actually made up of a connected series of ministories (scenes or sequences) which combine to make up larger blocks (acts or chapters) which combine to make up your work as a whole. A scene, the smallest dramatic unit, is really not different in its structure from a chapter or an act, and in turn, they are not different from your plot as a whole. Each has a beginning, a middle, and an end.

This means that you can employ the same strategy for each dramatic unit in your work. For example, decide what your objective is for a chapter *before* you write it. Then decide where you want to begin the telling.

Experience shows that if you've chosen a strong ending for your chapter, one which is both consistent with the work and dramatically effective, then you'll actually arrive at that point. If, however, you choose a weak end point, then you may very well "stray" from your intended path as the story progresses according to its own needs. *If you feel a strong current moving you away from your original objective, don't panic.* Go with the flow. Relax and let the story unfold. You'll know soon enough if this deviation is for better or for worse.

4. *Develop a working strategy.* Don't decide on a strategy for a chapter until you've written the chapter preceding it. If you're the sort of person who likes to map out an entire book, chapter by chapter, before you begin the actual writing, then be prepared to adapt to conditions as they change during the writing. You may alter course in ways that make your original plan for the book obsolete, or you may alter course in minor ways that don't really change the overall aim of the work. A working strategy constantly readjusts itself according to the changing conditions. Let's say, for instance, that your character Floyd, who's been a wallflower all along, suddenly decides against your better advice to get amorous, and you learn that underneath that

mashed potatoes exterior lies the heart of a red-hot lover. Then you should alter your strategy of character in order to accommodate this added dimension of Floyd's character.

5. *Don't ever look back.* Constantly looking back over your shoulder and worrying about whether what you've already written is good enough will not only cost you precious time, but it will divert your energy and attention. I've seen too many writers get hung up in the starting block. They don't think what they've written was good enough, so they go back and start over. And over. They'll keep starting over and rewriting the same material until they feel they've got it "right." As a result they never get very much past the starting line.

Writing takes enormous physical and mental effort. You need to focus your energy in one direction, not two. It's hard enough worrying about what to write next without having to worry about what you've written last. The temptation to go back is sometimes very strong and you must resist it, although there are times when something occurs to you and you *know* you have to get it down on paper or lose it. If this does happen, then you should give in to the impulse, but don't let yourself get caught in a rut that keeps getting deeper. Keep a notebook of ideas and changes for the work you've already written, but keep your eye on the horizon ahead of you.

Besides, if you do go back and spend hours or even days rewriting, the work may ultimately be wasted. You may realize later in the writing that the material you spent so much time making "right" really doesn't belong in the story after all, and you end up throwing it into the wastepaper basket. The time for making changes and for rewriting is after you've finished a first draft and you've begun to realize the actual nature of the work you've written. So complete the distance first. Your first draft is the first lap, the one that charts the course.

CHAPTER 2

PATTERN OF AUDIENCE

MYSTERY AND INTRIGUE

To understand the importance of pattern to fiction and the importance of strategy to pattern, we must take a few minutes to explain the role pattern plays between you, as the author, and the reader; because it is the success or failure of this relationship more than any other that will determine if your work will be successful.

We too often forget the nature of the relationship between writer and reader and take our audience for granted. We concentrate too much on the mechanics of writing and not enough on the critical process of reading. You can't hope to be a good writer until you understand the nature of the process that connects you and your work to the rest of the world. An arrogant attitude has developed among many writers in this century that they are above audience, that a work of literature must exist for itself and not for the people who might read it. They don't write for people, but for the page. This attitude is self-defeating. What good is a work of art if no one understands it? Every work needs an audience, even if that audience is only one person. John Steinbeck advised, "Your audience is a single reader. I have found that sometimes it helps to pick out one person—a real person you know, or an imagined person—and write to that one."

Don't make the mistake of treating your audience as a passive observer with no active part in your story. You tell, they listen. A story is a shared experience between author and reader. The reader wants to play an active role when he reads your work.

How is that possible?

Any fiction is a mystery. Not like the mysteries of Agatha Christie or Arthur Conan Doyle or Elmore Leonard, but similar to them in one important respect: Every story should offer a challenge to the reader in the form of a puzzle to be solved. We love the challenge of a good puzzle, and a good puzzle is one that is hard enough to test our skills of deduction but not so hard that we have no chance of solving it.

The classic murder mystery, such as Agatha Christie's *The Murder of Roger Ackroyd*, is the clearest example of literature that purposefully includes the reader as part of the story. The puzzle is clearly defined and the challenge is implied by the title of the book: who killed Roger Ackroyd? Miss Christie was very concerned with who the reader thought might be the culprit, because the novel's success depends on cleverly outwitting the reader. She made a career of guessing her readers' guesses and then staying one step ahead. The answer was always available, but only to those readers who could outguess Miss Christie. And even if you couldn't figure out the solution, you always felt the answer was right in front of you, cleverly disguised.

The main reason why mysteries sell so well is because their best writers are keenly aware of their readers and allow them to actively participate in trying to solve the crime. Devoted readers of the genre most look forward specifically to the challenge of solving the crime before the detective does. Not only do they feel included in the process, but they feel they're an important part of it.

The problem with many television detective shows today is that the audience is denied the clues necessary to solve the crime. Detectives from shows like *Columbo* and *B. L. Striker* and even the classic *Perry Mason* are more magician than sleuth: they're good at pulling rabbits out of the hat at the last minute. We're forced into the role of passive observers making wild guesses based on too little information. We aren't given a chance to figure out things for ourselves, and so we get little satisfaction at seeing the detective, who always has an unfair advantage, solve the puzzle. We've been cheated of the chance to participate. Don't make the mistake of treating your readers like deadheads. They want, *more than anything*, to be part of your work, to be given a chance to solve the mystery for themselves. So when you start your story, remember to keep your readers grasping at your coattails. Leave a trail of clues for them to follow, clues that make them think and wonder in what direction you're headed. Don't give away the answers, and don't make them so tough that no one could figure them out without a crystal ball.

If you've ever seen Orson Welles' *Citizen Kane*, you know the mystery of the film is to discover the meaning of Charles Foster Kane's dying word, "Rosebud." What does it mean? The newspaper editor assigns a reporter to find out what it means, and the reporter, like us, must try to find the answer.

The answer comes in the last minute of the film. Did the viewer have enough clues during the film to figure it out before then? Yes. There are about six major clues, each woven artfully into the story. None of the clues jumps out and bites you, but once you know the answer and go back over the film, they're easy to see. The answers are there, right before our eyes all along, but most of us didn't know how to read them. We were outsmarted, but in a satisfying way. For those who figured out the mystery, well, then they were sharper than the rest of us, but they also proved the mystery *could* be solved.

This thinking shouldn't be confined to the writing of mysteries. Every story, whether written by Jackie Collins or Larry McMurtry or James Michener, includes within it the same elements of mystery. Take Ernest Hemingway's *The Old Man and the Sea*, for example. It hardly belongs in the tradition of Dashiell Hammett or Raymond Chandler. It's a fishing story. An old man goes fishing for eighty-four straight days with no luck and on the eighty-fifth day hooks the biggest marlin ever seen. On the surface, *The Old Man and the Sea* is little more than an adventure story. So where's the mystery in that?

Think for a moment about the concept of intrigue. To intrigue means to arouse an interest, desire, or curiosity about something. As the writer you have the responsibility to create a sense of intrigue for the characters and the plot of your work. Without this intrigue, your reader loses interest.

Intrigue may express itself regarding the plot ("What's going to happen?") or the characters ("What's she going to say?") or even for the author's style (in the images or language, for instance). The intrigue in *The Old Man and the Sea* works on all these levels.

The mystery in *The Old Man and the Sea* expresses itself through the plot with a series of simple questions. The first question is obvious: "After eighty-four days without luck, will the old man catch anything today?" Thirty-six pages later Santiago sets his hook into what he knows must be a huge fish. The first question now changes focus to "Will the old man catch the great fish?" Sixty pages later Santiago wins his triumphant but exhausting three-day battle with the fish. But no sooner does he lash the 1800-pound fish to the side of his skiff than a mako shark attacks the carcass. The old man must now fight off wave after wave of frenzied sharks. The original question of whether or not Santiago was going to catch the fish now changes entirely to "Will the old man be able to keep his fish?"

These are the three successive plot movements in the novella. Each movement creates its own mystery, and each set of clues and solutions propels us forward.

If Hemingway had used a stereotypical old fisherman in his story, then he would have had to rely entirely on the intrigue of the plot to sustain the reader's attention. But Hemingway was a superior craftsman. He understood that the story would have no real meaning if it weren't for a character of substance. Santiago isn't a faceless cardboard cut-out who goes through the motions in order to make the plot happen. He is a man of complex emotions and motivations, and it is our fascination with him as a man that defines the nature of his great deed and the tragedy that follows. So just as the mystery that centers around the physical action of the plot unfolds, so does a series of parallel questions that deal with character. The questions that intrigue the reader about the old man parallel the same three movements of the plot. In the first movement we're curious about the old man's forty-day fast. He's weak and he's old. Will he survive this drought of luck?

At the same place the plot question changes (from "Will he catch anything?" to "Will he catch this huge fish?") our interest in Santiago changes from "Will he survive?" to "Will he survive this battle with the fish?" The twists of plot and character overlap, and so intensify the reader's experience.

The intrigues overlap again later in the book as the story moves into its third movement. Just as the plot question changes (from "Will he catch this huge fish?" to "Will he be able to save his catch?") so too the character intrigue changes its focus. We have watched the old man fight with gallantry and dignity to overcome the first two obstacles confronting him. But now, as the sharks devour his prize catch, the question becomes, "How will he endure this defeat?"

More careful readers also become intrigued with Hemingway's more subtle touches as they read beneath the surface of the story. A more sophisticated and subtler literary intrigue develops. Hemingway's descriptions of the old man are very Christ-like, which makes the reader wonder if there's a religious mystery hidden beneath the surface of the story. Santiago also falls into the tradition of Captain Ahab in *Moby Dick* and the Ancient Mariner in Samuel Taylor Coleridge's poem. Is he an epic hero? Or a tragic hero? Who is this old man?

A serious work of literature will spawn dozens of questions, each of them a mystery, each of them an intrigue, available to the reader to decipher.

In effect the author issues a challenge to the reader. Here are the people, and here are the events. Now, what's going to happen? This challenge is the single most exciting element in fiction because it's what spurs the reader on page after page, chapter after chapter. As soon as one question is answered, it's replaced by another and yet another, and so forth through the work.

In one sense reading is a contest between the author and the reader. The reader makes a guess about what will happen next, based upon his observations of the patterns of behavior of your characters and the patterns of events that affect them. Every good mystery has its clues, and clues add up to solutions if they're read properly. But as every mystery buff knows, interpreting clues *correctly* is the name of the game. Ralph Waldo Emerson once pointed out that it's a *good reader* that makes a good book.

THE COYOTE

Add to the concept of mystery the excitement of the chase. The chase is unique to literature and film, and it's one of its most provocative elements.

The chase has two players: the reader (the chaser) and the writer (the chased). The chase takes place on a course, which is the text of your story.

What's the object of the chase?

Logically the object of any chase is to catch that which you are pursuing. In this case, that means the reader tries to catch the writer by figuring out (based on his interpretation of clues) where the story is headed. The reader wins the chase.

Only he doesn't win.

This isn't a logical chase. If you make your clues too obvious, then the reader will have an easy time figuring out what's going to happen, and so the chase ends up with the reader ahead of the author. But instead of feeling victorious, the reader feels cheated because you haven't challenged him. You didn't give him a chance to savor the clues, collect details that make the pattern, and then decipher their meaning. When you're transparent, your readers will see through you every time.

Think back to the books you've read and the films you've seen in which the end was so obvious that you figured out everything that was going to happen halfway through the work. Remember how disappointed you were? Remember how angry you felt that you'd wasted your time and money on something that was so obvious? Remember how quickly you lost interest once you'd figured things out? The worst crime any writer can be accused of is that of predictability. Predictable is another way of saying boring. The reader finds the pattern too easy, too ordinary, because the mystery doesn't pose enough of a challenge.

In terms of the chase, the reader has won because he correctly predicted what was going to happen, but in a more profound sense, the reader has lost because he's been denied the pleasure of what he was looking for in the first place: surprise and intrigue.

This is what makes the chase so unique. Your reader is a very unusual opponent. On the one hand, he'll try very hard to outguess you, but on the other hand, no matter how hard he tries, he wants even more to be wrong.

Your responsibility as a writer is to make sure the reader gets a good run for his money. To do that, you have to tantalize your audience, and in order to tantalize your reader, you have to learn how to play a good game of cat and mouse. This is the essence of strategy.

Consider the three possible positions for the reader to be in during the chase:

1. The writer's always at a great advantage over the reader because he already knows every twist and turn in the course (after all, he created it!). The reader is at a disadvantage because he knows nothing about the course other than what he can guess about it, based on his skill of recognizing the patterns (clues) of the story. If the writer doesn't leave enough clues for the reader to make a theory about what's going to happen, then the writer is guilty of leaving the reader too far behind.

Let's say you're writing a story about Howard, a short-order cook in the diner where Elise works as a waitress. Howard is quiet, even secretive, and if it weren't for Elise's persistence, he would keep solely to himself. We watch Howard come out of his shell: his first date with Elise, their first kiss, and so on. But Howard won't talk about his past, and we decide he's hiding something. (A mystery!) Who is Howard, and what is he hiding?

Let's say, for the sake of argument, that on the eve of their marriage, Howard suddenly cancels the wedding.

"Why?" demands Elise.

"Because," Howard confesses his secret at last, "I'm an alien."

"You mean like from Mexico?"

"I mean like from outer space."

OH? you groan. *From outer space?*

You've lost the reader. Surprise endings that come from outer space like this one "alienate" the reader. No clues, no hints. Out-of-the-blue solutions are no solutions. The reader never had a chance. A chase is only exciting if the chaser has sight of his quarry. If the reader is left too far behind, and the trail becomes so confused that it becomes impossible to follow, then the reader will likely lose interest and give up the chase.

2. Conversely, if you let the reader catch up to you because you've made the trail too easy to follow, then he'll likely get bored and abandon the chase.

Back to Elise and Howard. Suppose during their first date Howard gets nervous when he sees a cop. And suppose in the next chapter, Elise finds out Howard is divorced and has their only child, a boy named Will. What conclusion would you reach? Howard has kidnapped his son from his wife. End of surprise. Too easy.

3. If, however, you construct a course that constantly keeps the reader off-balance, but one that allows the reader to always keep the writer in sight, then you've created the perfect chase. The pleasure of reading is in experiencing the unexpected twist of character or plot that keeps us guessing. Precisely at the moment when the reader thinks he knows what's going to happen, something else happens that upsets his theory and forces him to come up with a new one.

Elise and Howard again. Based on the clues we've had so far, we suspect Howard has grabbed his son and is in hiding. But in the next chapter we learn the mother is dead. So much for our theory. The plot question—what is Howard hiding from?—is alive again, and our interest is doubled.

In the next chapter we learn Howard's son is dying of cancer. A clue, but how does it fit? We're kept guessing. Finally Elise learns that Howard has escaped from prison so he can be with his son during his last days. Predictable? Not if you play your clues right, not if you tease your audience into making wrong guesses.

THE ROADRUNNER

If you've ever watched the classic cartoons of Wile E. Coyote and the Roadrunner, you know exactly what I'm talking about. The coyote is driven to catch the roadrunner, and he's always within an inch of grabbing his prey. But the roadrunner, which is a perfect metaphor for the writer, is never really in danger, because he's in complete control of himself *and* the coyote, despite the coyote's lamebrained schemes to catch him. What both relish more than anything is the chase. Both are defined by it. If coyote should one day catch the roadrunner, he'd probably get depressed and end up letting him go so the two could go back to what they love best: the chase.

So it is with the writer and the reader. The reader, the coyote, constantly comes within inches of grabbing the writer, the roadrunner, but every time he does, the roadrunner accelerates just enough to stay out of harm's way.

So, as your story develops from page to page, be careful not to give too much away. Don't delay information too long, either. Readers thrive on clues—they are the pieces of the puzzle. If you drag out the clues, your reader will get bored. And keep your clues ambiguous. They should suggest—as in the imaginary story with Elise and Howard—without stating emphatically.

In *Chinatown*, which takes place in Los Angeles during a drought in the thirties, almost every scene contains clues that deal with water. The solution of the central mystery of the film—who killed Hollis Mulwray?—has to do with water. Mulwray is drowned (ironically during a drought), and his murder is solved based upon evidence found in water. The clues are plentiful, and they don't give too much away. They are also ambiguous enough to keep us and the main character guessing. Even when the detective finds the evidence that solves the crime, he misinterprets it and accuses the wrong person.

How then can you achieve such a delicate and yet dangerous balance in the chase?

By developing an audience strategy.

Remember the following points:

1. The reader makes guesses about what's going to happen based upon *expectation*.
2. Expectation is the result of identifying and interpreting *patterns*.
3. Patterns are *designs* created by the writer.
4. Designs are the result of *strategy*.

As the roadrunner, you have three avenues available for you to create an audience strategy:

1. *Give the audience what it expects*. This strategy doesn't satisfy the audience, it frustrates it. If you give the reader what he expects, then your work lacks originality and is guilty of being predictable. The first step of figuring out a sound strategy, however, is to think out what you think the audience *does* expect. It is your starting point. In the story about Elise and Howard, the audience will expect that Howard has kidnapped his son.

2. *Give the audience the unexpected*. At first this sounds like a positive strategy, but it really isn't. This is the condition that causes the reader to fall too far behind the writer. If the patterns you have created are too complex or too bizarre or too incomplete to allow the reader a chance to participate, then you may end up losing your audience even more quickly than if you gave the reader what he expected. Readers just don't like twists that come "out of nowhere." The version of the Elise and Howard story in which Howard confesses he's an alien from outer space is an example.

3. *Give the audience what it expects, but not in the way it expects to get it*. This strategy combines the best of many worlds. The third version of the Elise and Howard story does this. First, it

satisfies the reader's anticipation of pattern.

Let me explain.

Whenever we see an incomplete pattern, our mind automatically tries to complete it. (Sometime watch the pleasure a child gets when playing a game of "Connect the Dots.") If I were to show you a half-finished drawing of an apple, you'd complete the drawing in your mind. You recognized the pattern of "apple" and successfully projected its conclusion.

This same process occurs when we read. We detect incomplete patterns, and on the basis of them, try to project a complete picture. What is any mystery but an incomplete pattern? Clues are fragments of the pattern, begging someone with a sharp eye and a sharp mind to solve the puzzle. This process is one of the most important in all of reading because we take pleasure in knowing we've correctly identified the patterns.

As a writer, you don't want to deny the reader this pleasure, but at the same time, you don't want to make the pattern so obvious that it loses its challenge. So you combine a portion of predictability with surprise. The predictability comes in the basic pattern, but the surprise comes in the original and unanticipated way you present that pattern.

For example, one of the most basic plots known to humanity is the revenge plot. It's a very simple and yet very compelling plot that never loses its appeal.

The basic plot progression is familiar to everyone: an injustice is committed against an innocent person (usually murder) and another person (usually a family member or a lover) sets out to even the score. The pattern is as old as literature itself. The reader knows the plot so well that he finds it easy to guess what's going to happen. Anyone who's seen any of Sergio Leone's spaghetti Westerns (the ones with Clint Eastwood such as *Hang 'Em High*, *Fistful of Dollars*, and *For a Few Dollars More*) knows the formula by heart.

Up to a point.

Let's take a closer look at the idea of pattern.

Look at this figure:

What is it?

A pie with a slice cut out? A Pac-Man? Those are the obvious answers. If I were to say, yes, it's a pie with a slice cut out of it, then you'd shrug your shoulders and say "So?"

What if I added a second figure to the first:

and again asked you, "What is it?"

The puzzle is changed with the addition of the second clue. The mind has to rethink the problem. I have created a chain of events: first, the figure at the top, and second, the figure on the bottom left. The figures are the same, yet they face in different directions (clue). The original question of "What is it?" now adds to it the question, "What is the connection between the two?" Another way of looking at the problem: The first figure is "A" and the second figure is "B." "A" + "B" = ?

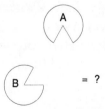

This is the essence of pattern in fiction. Point "A" in a story leads to point "B." "A" and "B" then combine to suggest to the reader "C."

What is "C" in the puzzle above?

"C" is strongly suggested by the combination of "A" and "B." In this case "C" is so strongly suggested by "A" and "B" that it becomes the obvious and compelling result (choice) because it completes the pattern:

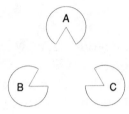

Why is this the obvious and compelling choice?

Because it is the only satisfying answer. The answer appeals to our sense of geometric symmetry and our sense of logic. The addition of the third figure completes the third corner of an "invisible" triangle which exists in the blank space between the three figures:

But the pattern doesn't really exist! The triangle isn't really there. However it is suggested by the placement of the three figures. But the suggestion is so strong that it's inescapable.

Let's look at some alternative solutions.

Suppose I'd placed the third figure in this position instead:

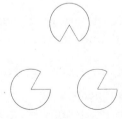

The "answer" doesn't satisfy. We sense something is wrong, that the figure is placed incorrectly, that it violates the pattern implicit in the figures. Our sense of pattern is so strong that our mind wants to "correct" the third figure by making it conform to the internal logic of the puzzle.

Suppose the third figure was a square:

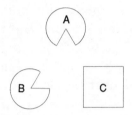

This too doesn't satisfy. In fact it's downright mystifying. The audience is likely to respond with a "Huh?" The square is a major violation of the internal logic of the puzzle and offers no satisfying solution at all. It offers confusion and perhaps anger. We demand an explanation. And even if I could give you one (which I can't), you still wouldn't feel satisfied. As readers we get enjoyment in completing patterns and feeling the sense of completeness that goes with a whole. The other two solutions—if they can be called that—do not lend themselves to a sense of completeness or wholeness.

As a writer you want to work within established patterns and wholes because they are your common ground with the audience. You offer incomplete patterns which suggest strongly what might happen next, and as in the figure above, you make your readers see the "invisible" triangle. You make them see what doesn't exist. Of course the symbols of language (words) are much more complex and varied than the simple symbol in the puzzle above, but that's what gives your puzzle so many possibilities, rather than the one solution available for this puzzle.

This concept of implication is the bulk of the writer's arsenal. Just as the first two figures in the puzzle above imply the existence of the third figure in order to complete the pattern, so you, as the creator of a more complex puzzle, supply pieces of that puzzle to the reader so he is driven to make conclusions based upon inescapable implications.

The difference between this simple logic puzzle and a story is in its complexity. The simple puzzle has two simple clues that create a strong but single implication. A story, however, has perhaps dozens of clues that may create several strong implications. The audience is likely to choose the most obvious implication, and that's the one you should avoid. But you shouldn't avoid it entirely: use it as your point of departure. Don't be predictable. Surprise the reader with something unexpected, something that, upon looking back over the clues, causes the reader to say, "Yes, of course, I see it now," just as the clues in *Citizen Kane* tell us what "Rosebud" means.

DESIGNING A STRATEGY

Anticipation, pattern, and strategy. Three elements of storytelling that ensure your audience stays glued to the page.

With these in mind, you should design a strategy with the following goals:

1. *A strategy should be process- as well as goal-oriented.* Don't make the mistake of concentrating solely on the "punchline" or goal of your story. This mistake is commonly made by many writers who feel that the telling of the story isn't as important as the final twist at the end. When you hear the name of O. Henry (William Porter), you ordinarily think of his short story "The Gift of the Magi," which has perhaps the most famous surprise ending of any short story. In a marvelous twist that creates a perfect balance (pattern), the young lady cuts and sells her hair in order to buy a gold fob for her husband's watch, who meanwhile sells his watch to buy an ivory comb for her hair.

"The Gift of the Magi" is considered a model of the surprise ending, and O. Henry is considered a master of the form. But sit down and try to read an entire volume of O. Henry stories.

The exquisiteness of "The Gift of the Magi" fades rapidly when you have to read story after story after story with the same formula. You find yourself skipping to the end, impatient for the twist.

The reason for the impatience is obvious. O. Henry put too much emphasis on the goal (the surprise ending) and not enough emphasis on the telling of the story itself. Keep in mind that reading is a process. Have you ever noticed how wearisome one-line jokes become when you have to listen to a bunch of them at once? The telling isn't funny (it usually comes in the form of a question), only the punchline, and then not always. The really good jokes we remember are the ones that made us laugh *before* the teller got to the punchline. They were funny in the beginning, in the middle, and at the end. They were process-oriented as well as goal-oriented.

Good writing is the same. While a reader should look forward to what's going to happen next, the reader should also enjoy where he is at the moment in the text. The work is a series of puzzles (questions that beg answers) and an accumulation of clues.

2. *Be aware of the reader's expectations.* A good writer tries to anticipate what the reader is thinking and feeling. Of course different readers have different expectations, and no two readers are exactly alike, but you can decide what is the most obvious expectation of your average reader. Keep in mind John Steinbeck's advice to write with one specific person in mind; this will help you focus on your audience as someone particular rather than a huge, faceless mass of people. Of course some of your readers will always figure out what you're doing—you can't fool all the people all the time—but if you can trick the person for whom you're writing, then you will succeed with most of your audience if you've chosen your "typical," "ideal" reader well. Based upon what is the obvious, develop your story and your characters in ways that are still consistent with the pattern (in order to allow the reader the pleasure of tracing the pattern), but different enough to be refreshing, original, and surprising.

3. *Present a unified experience.* The reader wants answers. A reader also wants a final reckoning. Unlike life, which often stub-

bornly refuses to give answers, you are accountable for person and event in your story. No major unanswered questions, no clues unaccountable, no characters left hanging. All the pieces are in place and they all fit.

We sometimes get caught up in our own stories and forget to give all the important answers: Why did your character act that way? What ever happened to . . . ? Motives should be clear and events should be resolved. The reader should have no questions left. The pattern should be made complete.

Elvis Presley called this stage "takin' care of business." A story is a tapestry, and a tapestry is made up of hundreds of threads. Any threads that are left dangling detract from the pattern and distract the story. But when everything "fits," we are left with a sense of wholeness and completeness. This feeling is the most satisfying of all, for both writer and reader.

CHAPTER 3

PATTERN IN STRUCTURE

ALL ABOUT ORIGINALITY

We live under the mistaken impression that "originality" means that when we sit down to write, we must create everything out of whole cloth. "Borrowing" is forbidden. We read in the papers about the endless stream of suits being filed in every court in the land charging such-and-such an author with stealing from other works.

An interesting but by no means atypical case in July 1986 serves as an illustration. Morris Albert, author of the pop song "Feelings," was hauled into court by Louis Gaste, who claimed that the song was pirated directly from his obscure French cafe song, "Pour Toi," which he'd written over twenty years earlier. A Manhattan federal court jury agreed with Gaste and awarded him half a million dollars in damages.

Even former Beatle George Harrison had to pay $400,000 in damages because a judge decided that his song "My Sweet Lord" sounded too much like the Chiffons' 1963 hit single "He's So Fine" ("Doo lang, doo lang, doo lang").

A hundred years ago such suits were unheard of. Would Smetana have sued Puccini for stealing the opening of *Madame Butterfly* from the overture of *The Bartered Bride*? Or would Beethoven have sued Wagner for stealing the opening of the "Prize Song" from *Die Meistersinger* from Beethoven's *Ninth Symphony*? I doubt it. Borrowing was a common and respected practice. More importantly, these artists recognized that borrowing

33

is inescapable. Our ideas must come from somewhere; they don't just come out of thin air. Brahms borrowed from Handel, Tchaikovsky borrowed from Mozart, and Bach borrowed from Vivaldi. No shame, because there was no crime.

We think of Shakespeare as the greatest writer in the English language and yet of his thirty-six plays *not one* was an original story. (To be perverse, one might say William Shakespeare was the greatest *rewriter* in the English language.) The same is true of Chaucer and Milton and Spenser. They took existing stories and reworked them. Under our present legal system, English literature's greatest writers would all be found guilty of plagiarism in a court of law.

Author George Moore pointed out the real difference between stealing and borrowing: "Taking something from one man and making it worse," he said, "is plagiarism." Certainly Shakespeare and Chaucer and Spenser were innocent of that crime.

The point is that we all make trips to the trough of literature to drink our fill. (Ralph Waldo Emerson said, "[everyone] is a borrower and a mimic, life is theatrical and literature a quotation.") Even Monsieur Gaste, who won his suit against Morris Albert, was himself guilty of taking his inspiration for "Pour Toi" from Verdi's *La Traviata*. And so 'round and 'round it goes.

Of course Chaucer and Shakespeare didn't have copyright law to worry about. Stories were always considered within the public domain and everyone had the right to use any one he wanted. Today, with our laws that favor the exclusive rights of personal property, much of the vast repertoire of stories has been "claimed" by authors under the copyright laws of the United States and other countries. This state of events has created the false impression among beginning writers that any story you create must be totally original. Add to that the stigma that if you do resort to a story that is already familiar to audiences, then you will almost certainly be accused of stealing.

This view is obviously hypocritical. We praise our great authors, all of whom were thieves according to our new standards of judgment, and then we criticize contemporary authors for lacking originality when they do the same thing. The truth is that we all look to other sources for our inspiration. Today we have to be much cagier about our "thefts" then were our forebears, a state of affairs that led the American playwright William Inge to define originality as "undetected plagiarism."

By plagiarism Inge didn't mean stealing another author's work word for word. He was referring to the primal pool of stories that have been circulating since the beginning of literature itself. We applaud Homer's *The Odyssey* as one of the great creative works of Western literature, and yet we know Homer didn't make up the story, that he merely conveyed an existing story in the public tradition of oral storytellers. What made Homer great is the style he brought to the story. "Nothing is new," historian Will Durant pointed out, "except arrangement."

How then does a writer today overcome these handicaps regarding originality? First you should realize that it's impossible to create the totally original plot with totally original characters. And if you did somehow manage to create a totally original work, it would be so alien to human experience that no one would understand what you were talking about. The task to come up with "new" material isn't just difficult, it's impossible. If you try to come up with a story that's never been told before — which is the implicit responsibility of writers according to current attitudes — then you put yourself in a vacuum by cutting yourself off from the thousands of years of human experience. More experienced writers know they have to rely on all the writers and thinkers that have preceded them. If everything has been thought of before, then our job as writers is to think of it again for our people in our time.

Some of our century's best talents have looked to the past for their inspiration. Recent stage musicals make the point: Leonard Bernstein's *West Side Story* (from *Romeo and Juliet*), Andrew Lloyd Weber's *Phanthom of the Opera*, Stephen Sondheim's *Into the Woods* (from "Little Red Riding Hood"), and many other works, from Hugo's *Les Misérables* and to Kafka's *Metamorphosis*.

I included this discussion about originality in this chapter on pattern in structure because the stories that we have been drawing on for thousands of years themselves constitute what I shall call the pattern of literature itself. By the time we're adults, we're completely versed in this pattern of literature, and as readers we come to expect it in the books we read and the films we see. The pattern is so deeply ingrained within us that we can hardly think of any other kind of literature. From the moment we are born we begin to hear stories, and we don't stop hearing them until the moment we die. As children we hear (and see) them in the form of songs, lullabies, fables, jokes, parables, and tales. As adults we hear, read, and see the same stories in the form of operas, ballets, stage dramas, and films. The vehicle bearing the story becomes more sophisticated as we grow older, but the stories stay the same.

This isn't to say we lack imagination and can't come up with anything new after five thousand years of trying. What it does say is that there are certain patterns of thinking, writing, and reading that remain constant because they are the root of human experience. They have entered our unconscious mind and become part of us. We all know the basic cast of characters that don't change from century to century, just as we know the basic plots, which haven't changed since the beginning of literature.

These aren't things we have to go to school to learn. Karl Jung called these fundamental characters and plots (and images and sounds) *archetypes*. The Old Wise Man and the Great Mother, for instance, are basic to all people whether it's someone walking down 57th Street in Manhattan today or someone crawling beneath the jungle canopy in New Guinea ten thousand years ago. We have shared these images, sounds, and concepts for tens of thousands of years, and so when you sit down by yourself at the kitchen table with a pen in your hand, you actually draw from this well of shared experience that lives in your unconscious mind. But because you can't see it, and because you can't put your hands on it, you tend to mistrust it. You feel isolated when you write. Alone. No one to lean on. But in fact you have the shared experience of humanity and civilization inside yourself. And this content expresses itself in the basic patterns of character and plot.

Which brings up my second point. Don't divorce yourself from the traditional patterns of literature because of society's false (and shallow) attitude that all new works must be totally original works in order to be considered "good." The pattern of literature itself, whether in the form of fairy tale or fable or myth or parable—whatever form it takes—is fundamental not only to the writer but also to the reader. We rely on those patterns, no matter how much we may deny it. Call it imitation, call it plagiarism, call it whatever you want, but no writer should apologize or feel he is "cheating" just because he looks to the past for inspiration. On the contrary, what you're doing is joining the literary present with the literary past and continuing its tradition.

Voltaire expressed this sentiment when he remarked, "Originality is nothing but judicious imitation. The most original writers borrowed from one another. The instruction we find in books is like fire. We fetch it from our neighbors, kindle it at home, communicate it to others, and it becomes the property of all."

The pattern of literature isn't something you have to search far and wide in order to find: it surrounds us. You'll find it in the simplest of children's stories, in nursery rhymes, in folk tales and folk legends, and in the classical myths of any culture. Read them. Don't be deceived by their simplicity; they're the kernel of all literature.

Structure is itself archetypal. We instinctively understand the three-part structure of beginning, middle, and end. We understand the rhythm and the feel of the pattern. Leave off or distort any one of the three and the story won't feel right. Writers have often tried to break away from this ancient concept of structure, but without success, mainly because no one has ever come up with a suggestion of what to replace it with. And so, for better or worse, we write in this formula—beginning, middle, and end.

In the Beginning

The beginning is not necessarily where you start. You may start writing the story in the middle or the end, but eventually you will have to go back and write the beginning. The beginning should accomplish certain objectives.

1. Establish character(s). Introduce them one at a time or in *small* groups, so the reader becomes comfortable with them. Don't force your entire roster of characters on the reader at once; that will confuse him. A lot of us have a hard time getting into nineteenth-century Russian novels because the authors love to present twenty or thirty people in as many pages. We need a character flow chart to keep track of who's who. Don't bunch major and minor characters together; important characters first.

The best method for introducing characters is to introduce them through other characters rather than directly by the author. A wonderful example comes from *Madame Bovary*, on the first page. Flaubert is about to introduce Charles Bovary, one of the main characters of the novel. But Flaubert knew readers accept characters much more readily if they are introduced to us through other characters, so he invented a schoolboy who's sitting in a classroom watching the boy Charles walk into the classroom for the first time.

The boy's description of Charles tells us a lot about Charles' character: the way he dresses and acts. Charles is vivid and the scene is alive, rather than having a narrator give us all these same details secondhand. Flaubert then dumps the schoolboy after the first page and we never see him again. His purpose is only to introduce the main character.

Don't force the character on the reader. Give us time to know him or her; don't take too long either. Readers are impatient for action. But since action is character, what the character does also tells us who he/she is.

2. Establish place. Stories have to happen somewhere. Chapter 8 tells you how to do this, but for now, immediately give your characters ground to walk on, places to go, and things to see. Don't leave your characters in a vacuum. *Jane Eyre, Wuthering Heights*, and *The Adventures of Huckleberry Finn* all plunge you into the place, which is as important as the characters.

3. Start action. Don't delay the story by giving descriptions of your characters or your setting. Characters say and do, and this is the beginning of the action in your story. The beginning

is responsible for setting up the dramatic premise of the story. Raise the central question of the story. (In *Citizen Kane* it's "What does 'Rosebud' mean?" and in *The Old Man and the Sea* it's "Will the old man catch his fish?") These questions get answered in the end, but for now they give the reader a puzzle to ponder, and a direction to pursue. The question can be simple, as it is in *Jaws* (Will Martin kill the shark?) or it may be complicated (Will Raskolnikov find meaning in life? — *Crime and Punishment*), but the point is that the question establishes the framework (the structure) for the story.

4. Start the story late. An airplane must taxi down the runway before it can get off the ground. Stories should begin at the moment they take off the ground; don't make us wade through pages of backstory while you taxi down the runway trying to get up enough speed to get airborne. *Kramer vs. Kramer* begins at the moment Meryl Streep's character leaves her husband. *Citizen Kane*, like Tolstoy's *The Death of Ivan Ilych*, begins with the death of the main character. Starting late gets the reader involved immediately.

5. Establish the tone. Comedy? Tragedy? Melodrama? What kind of story are you telling? Give us a feel of the style: breezy, comic, brooding, somber, silly, whatever. The first page of *The Maltese Falcon* and the first page of *Love Story* have an entirely different feel. Dostoyevsky's *Notes from Underground* feels different from *Duck Soup*.

Middles

Compared to beginnings and ends, middles are hard. The middle of your story is where things get complicated. What seemed predictable becomes unpredictable. This is the territory of the unexpected twist, the wrinkle, and the reversal. Characters run into barriers and obstacles that keep them from getting where they want to go. And just as the reader gets his sense of balance in terms of what's going to happen, you suddenly pull the rug from under him. In *American Graffiti*, for instance, the character played by Richard Dreyfuss spends the first act (the beginning) partying and goofing off prior to his departure for college. But then in the second act (the middle), the character sees the beautiful girl (played by Suzanne Sommers) in the T-Bird, which alters everything he does for the rest of the film as he searches for her. In *All the President's Men*, Woodward and Bernstein seek to uncover the Watergate burglary, but they run into difficulties when they find half of Washington, including the White House, is doing what it can to stop them from finding anything out. Whatever your character's problems are (as they were presented to us in the beginning), intensify them in the middle. Don't run your story in a straight line. Dips, valleys, ridges, rises, and falls keep the reader off-balance and on an unpredictable yet exciting ride through your story.

At Last

The end of your story is its resolution. The character solves his problems for better or for worse. It is the home of the climax, the big finish. The characters have their revelations; they learn what their struggle is about. Michael Corleone, who has been avoiding being involved in his family's business, becomes the new Godfather. Hamlet, sent on a mission of revenge, is forced to confront himself, with tragic results. Cinderella gets her prince and finds happiness. The end is the bottom line, the sum of both beginning and middle, and like a mathematical equation, everything must add up.

THE WHITE SNAKE

The most enduring form of popular literature in the world is the fairy tale. Every culture cherishes its fairy tales. We normally associate them with children, although critics such as Bruno Bettelheim and Max Luthi have pointed out that their effect reaches well beyond childhood into adulthood. Much of our own adult literature is based upon the same basic values and ideas that fairy tales put forth. As adults we simply dress the tales up in more sophisticated clothes, but underneath much of our world's literature lie the simple and elegant fairy tales and their complex notions of morality and socialization.

It is virtually impossible to live in North America or Europe and not know the stories of "Cinderella," "Sleeping Beauty," or "Little Red Riding Hood." As children, we hear the stories read to us by our parents, we see them animated in cartoons and feature-length films, we see them replayed in opera and ballet and on the stage, and again in films and novels of the day where they constantly change shape but remain essentially the same.

Fairy tales have a strong hold on our imagination because of their universality of pattern and their simplicity of structure. The success of the fairy tale relates to the fact that it has had centuries to refine its story, whereas we, as authors working alone, have at best a few years. A story repeated millions of times to children at the laps of their mothers over five hundred or a thousand years is bound to refine its structure.

Nowhere else can the influence of pattern in structure be seen so clearly as in the fairy tale. It represents storytelling in a basic, yet highly refined state.

"The White Snake" tale is simple and told in three parts (beginning, middle, and end). The story tells of a King who has strange powers of knowledge, which he gets from eating the meat from a magical white snake. The boy who delivers the King his snake every night succumbs to temptation and tastes the meat and finds out he can now understand the language of animals. At the same time, the Queen accuses the youth of stealing a gold ring from her. The King tells the boy that unless he can point out the thief by the next day, he will die.

The boy, who knows nothing, sits down next to a pond to try to figure out his troubles when he overhears the ducks in the pond talking among themselves. One duck has a stomach ache. "I don't feel so good," the duck complains. "I accidentally ate the Queen's gold ring today."

The youth grabs the duck and takes it to the cook to prepare for dinner, and lo and behold, the cook finds the ring inside the duck.

The King, feeling guilty for accusing his loyal servant, grants him any wish: a title, money, whatever he wants. But the youth, who wants to go out and see the world, asks only a horse and some travel money.

On his journey he comes across another pond where he hears three fish who are tangled in the reeds calling for help. He saves the fish, who cry out to him, "We will repay you for saving us!"

A while farther the youth then comes across a column of ants in the road that are cursing all the people who keep stepping on them. The youth carefully sidesteps the ants, and the ant-king, grateful for the youth's act of charity, promises, "One good turn deserves another!"

Next the youth comes across some newborn ravens who are starving in the nest. The youth kills his horse for meat and feeds them, and the grateful ravens repeat the refrain of the ants, "One good turn deserves another!"

The youth, now without a horse, walks to a great city where he learns that the King's daughter is looking for a husband. But in order to get the hand of the Princess, her suitor must first perform a difficult task or else lose his life. When the youth sees the Princess he decides he has to try to win her hand in marriage and so he submits to the test.

The test is difficult. The King throws a gold ring into the ocean and orders the youth to keep diving for it until he either finds the ring or drowns.

But the three fish whom the youth had saved earlier come to his rescue and bring the ring to him. He takes the ring to the King expecting to get the hand of the Princess in marriage, but the Princess, who doesn't want to marry a commoner, has other plans and demands that the youth submit to another test. Still infatuated, he agrees.

The Princess scatters ten sacks of millet seed on the grass and gives the youth until dawn to pick up all the seeds or he'll be put to death. At a loss, he is about to give up when the ants arrive and pick up all ten bags of seed for him.

The Princess, amazed by the youth's performance, decides to try one more time and this time orders him to find her an apple from the Tree of Life.

He travels out among many lands and kingdoms in search of the Tree of Life but can't find it. He is about to give up when the three young ravens whom he'd saved from starvation drop a golden apple from the Tree of Life into his hand.

The youth returns to the Princess with the golden apple. She falls in love with the youth after she shares the golden apple with him, they marry, and as the story says, "lived in undisturbed happiness to a great age."

The explicit moral of the tale is that if you help others, they will help you in your moment of need. The implicit moral is less obvious but no less important: there is no "ledger of debt" in helping people. A good deed is done for its own sake, not to create a debt owed. The young man doesn't look for or expect help from those whom he has helped; he is rewarded specifically because he *doesn't* expect the fishes, the ants, and the ravens to repay his kindnesses to them.

But I am less interested in the psychological and sociological implications of the tale than in how the tale itself is constructed and how it works in relation to its audience.

The structure of "The White Snake" is typical of fairy tales and stories in general. I chose it over the more familiar tales because it is less likely to distract you from an analysis of its form. (I am often amazed by the number of people who don't know the real fairy tales. Instead, they know the popular corruptions of them, which range from Walt Disney to Shelley DuVall's film productions for pay television.)

The story is told in fifteen paragraphs that divide into three movements, which make up its structure.

The first movement (the first four paragraphs) sets up the premise of the story.

In the first paragraph, we learn of a King who seems to know everything. We also learn of the mysterious dish that is brought to him in great secrecy every day after dinner. The reader has no trouble connecting the mysterious dish as the probable source of his superhuman knowledge. But the first paragraph teases us, makes us curious: what is in the dish? From our past experience with fairy tales, we suspect it must be something marvelous.

The second paragraph introduces the main character, a youth in faithful service to the King, who, like us, can't contain his curiosity and so sneaks a peek (and a taste) of the forbidden dish. The youth hears the sparrows outside the window chattering and suddenly understands their tongue. The last sentence of the paragraph states the premise of the tale: "Eating the snake had given him power of understanding the language of animals."

With the premise established, the third paragraph moves the story into its first crisis: The Queen has lost her ring and the youth stands unfairly accused. He faces the penalty of death if the ring isn't returned.

But his newfound knowledge allows him to eavesdrop on a flock of ducks in the fourth paragraph, and he learns that one of the ducks has swallowed the Queen's ring, thus allowing him to solve the first mystery of the story (who took the Queen's ring?). The crisis is solved; the first movement is over.

Note the simplicity of the pattern. The something hidden in paragraph one is discovered in paragraph two. The crisis that occurs in paragraph three (the Queen's lost ring) is resolved in paragraph four by the youth's use of his newfound knowledge. In terms of our expectations as readers, we can predict safely that this is only the beginning, and that he will encounter further difficulties as a result of this knowledge.

The second movement of the story begins in the fifth paragraph when the King grants the youth a favor for his loyalty. The youth chooses to go out into the world where he immediately encounters fishes tangled in reeds. The fishes promise to repay him for saving them. The youth then encounters the ant-king in paragraph six and the ravens in paragraph seven, all of whom he helps, and all of whom promise to repay his kindness.

The pattern that had been established in the first movement (and our experiences with other tales) makes us anticipate just how these animals will figure again in the life of the youth. The original question of the first movement (will the youth be able to prove his innocence?) has now changed to the question of the second movement (what's going to happen to him? And how will these animals help?).

The story enters the third and final movement. We expect a crisis more critical than the one in the first movement to occur, and we expect that the animals in the second movement will come to the youth's rescue.

Sure enough, he becomes infatuated with the beautiful Princess in paragraph eight. But the privilege to marry the King's daughter isn't for the asking: the youth must first prove himself by accomplishing a difficult task. This task is described in paragraph nine: he must retrieve a gold ring from the sea or die trying.

The immediate question becomes: how will he ever find the ring? But we know he has already been successful in finding lost rings (from the first movement) and we suspect that the fishes will come to his aid. Indeed they do, although the youth himself has no expectation that they will. The task now solved, he expects the hand of the Princess in marriage.

But the youth has yet to prove himself to the Princess, and she herself makes a second and more difficult demand in the eleventh paragraph: to pick up ten sacks-full of millet seed before sunrise without missing one or suffer the penalty of death.

Again the youth is in a quandary, and again, without expecting help, he gets it, this time from the ant-king, who has his people collect the seeds and return them to the sacks. We sensed this solution by tracing the pattern, and it happened. We also sense that another task is coming, this one more difficult than either of the two preceding it. Our expectation is that the story will continue to follow the pattern: that the ravens will come to the youth's rescue at his greatest moment of need.

The Princess, too haughty to accept a commoner for her husband, sets the third and final task in paragraph thirteen. Rather than force her suitor to engage in such mundane tasks as diving for gold rings or picking up millet seed, the Princess proposes a task that she believes no mortal could accomplish: to retrieve an apple from the Tree of Life.

In paragraph fourteen the youth goes out into the world without a clue about how to find, much less retrieve, an apple from the Tree of Life. He wanders aimlessly across three kingdoms until he stops, exhausted and hopeless, to rest beneath a tree, when suddenly the Golden Apple literally drops into his hand. Sure enough, the ravens, now grown, had flown to the end of the world to find the apple and bring it to the youth in order to repay the debt of gratitude for saving their lives.

In the final paragraph the youth returns to the Princess and presents her with the Golden Apple. We expect that the Princess will no longer be able to resist him and that the two will marry and live in interminable happiness. They do, of course, but not before they cut the apple in two and share it. Only then does the Princess' heart become "full of love for him."

"The White Snake" embodies a pattern of the quest that's basic not only to fairy tales but to all literature: the hero who sets forth into the unknown in search of the strongest, the most beautiful, or the most valuable. He encounters difficulties and must overcome them, and each difficulty he encounters is more vexing than the last. This is the story of Odysseus and Hercules and thousands of other heroes in literature. Their stories are essentially the same although the tasks themselves differ. It is the story of the voyage to maturity, to greatness, and it is the story of the Self.

The character of the youth, as well as the characters of the two Kings and the Princess, are purposefully kept at the simplest common denominator so as to keep the action uncomplicated and as universalized as possible. As a result we concentrate on events rather than the people, and we concentrate upon the meaning of those events. Because the characters of the youth and Princess are kept so simple, we can easily recognize the patterns of their behavior and project them. We know intuitively that the youth will continue to strive toward his goal whatever the penalty for failure, and we know that the Princess will not give in to the youth without first testing him to the limits.

A child unfamiliar with fairy tales may indeed wonder if the boy will get the girl, but from our experience with other fairy tales, we know "The White Snake" will have a happy ending. The question for us is not whether the boy will get the hand of the Princess but *how* he will get her hand.

All of this is accomplished in a total of fifty-four sentences. (Twenty in the first movement; thirteen in the second; and twenty-one in the third.) And, even with its simple structure and its minimum number of sentences, each of the three movements contains within it a beginning, a middle, and an end:

Movement I:

Beginning: The youth eats the snake and learns the language of animals.

Middle: The Queen loses her ring and the King accuses the youth of stealing it.

End: The youth finds the ring and establishes his innocence.

Movement II:

Beginning: The youth goes out into the world and saves the stranded fishes.

Middle: The youth spares the lives of the ants.

End: The youth rescues the starving ravens.

Movement III:

Beginning: The youth falls in love with the Princess and decides to become a suitor.

Middle: The youth must perform three tasks, one for the King and two for the Princess.

End: The youth gets the hand of the Princess in marriage.

The cause and effect relationship between events that constitute plot is straightforward and uncomplicated. To succeed the fairy tale relies heavily upon the reader's experience with pattern. If you've ever noticed the delight with which a child tries to guess the progression of events in a fairy tale, then you understand what a powerful force pattern brings to a narrative, and how it captures the imagination of the reader.

Pattern in structure also captures the imagination of the writer. You may argue that fairy tales are simplistic and not truly representative of adult literature, which is much more complex. True, the simplicity of the fairy tale (which is part of its charm) lacks many of the qualities of adult literature, (such as character development, for instance) but it would be a serious mistake to underestimate the impact this type of literature has on our own adult literature.

The fairy tale is closely related to myth; in fact, they are very nearly opposite sides of the same coin. The motif of prophecy in "Sleeping Beauty" (when the thirteenth witch cries out, "The princess shall in her fifteenth year be pricked by a spindle and fall down dead") and the prophecy in *Oedipus the King* (which forecasts he will murder his father and marry his mother) play the same role: they set up a familiar pattern and create expectation. Ask yourself why it is that we repeat the same basic stories over the centuries. Is the reason because we can't think of anything new and so reuse the old stories? Or is the reason more profound: are these stories—these patterns of behavior and concern—so fundamental to people that it makes no difference where or when they were born?

CHAPTER 4

PATTERN IN PLOT

THE WALRUS AND THE CARPENTER

In life, events follow one another for no apparent reason. You wake up in the morning to find out the power is off, and when you call the electric company to complain, the clerk tells you that you were disconnected because you didn't pay your bill on time. Only you *did* pay it on time, and you have the cancelled check to prove it. And while you're sitting at the table over a cup of coffee with your anger brewing on a slow simmer, your dog, which in ten years has never bitten anyone, decides to take a chunk out of the leg of the UPS man.

Why do these things happen?

They do, that's all. No rhyme, no reason. Those among us who are religious explain the haphazard order of life by citing God's "mysterious plan," and those among us who aren't religious shrug our shoulders and say it's blind chance. Who knows what got into the circuits of the electric company's computer? Who knows what got into your dog? The answers rarely ever come. Perhaps that's why we sympathize so much with Alice when she can't figure out why anything happens the way it does in Wonderland. The total lack of logic infuriates her whenever she tries to make sense of the topsy-turvy world through the looking-glass.

When it comes to logic, fiction isn't at all like life. Events in a story don't happen by chance. In fiction every event must *logically* follow another. (Don't you wish you could say that about your own life?) Life at times is chaotic, but fiction is always well-ordered.

The British novelist E. M. Forster made the difference between plot and story very clear: "The King died and then the Queen died," he said, was a story, not a plot. They are two events that aren't connected causally. We don't know *why* the Queen died. Did she choke on a piece of meat? Eat a poisoned apple? Did her death have *anything* to do with the King's death? Maybe, but we just don't know, because no solid connection is made between the two events.

Consider "The King died and then the Queen died *of grief.*" Now we have the makings of a plot. The Queen's death is a direct result of the King's death. The two events are bound together by cause (the King's death) and effect (the Queen's death as a result of her grief). This link between events is what creates plot.

A plot, then, is made up of events, but events in themselves do not necessarily make up a plot. (This is like saying all butterflies are insects but not all insects are butterflies.) The important point to remember, however, is that plot is a *pattern* of events.

How do you create such a pattern of events?

Think of yourself, the writer, as an architect. When you write, you need to design a structure that is at the same time logical, useful, and appealing to the eye and the mind. You will decide on a design and then *pursue* that design from beginning to end. We don't appreciate an architect who starts a design that's American Colonial and then suddenly switches in midstream to a house that looks like it was designed by Pablo Picasso during a nightmare. Experience (the recognition of pattern by repetition) has taught us to expect certain relationships to occur within the house: that there will be more bedrooms than kitchens, for instance, or that the bathrooms will be near the bedrooms. These are our expectations, and they are so deeply ingrained in us and our way of living that any house that dramatically violates this pattern is bound to go unsold for a long time. (For Sale: Modern Contemporary: 1 BR, 3 Kitchens, 5 baths.) Therefore, when you write, you should keep a master plan in mind as you develop the blueprint for your work.

As you begin work, you need to develop a sense of the web

of connections between people, places, and events. The people represent the pattern of characters, the places represent the pattern of settings, and the events represent the pattern of plot. These patterns can't really be separated from one another because each one in turn constantly affects the others: what a character *does* (plot) affects what he *says* (dialogue), just as where a character *is* (setting) affects what he *does*, which affects what he *says* . . . and so on.

The example of Edgar Allan Poe's story, "The Cask of Amontillado" gives us a clear view of the use of strategy in the development of plot. The story, written in 1846, at the very beginning of the modern short story as we know it, is very purposeful and direct for its length (it's only 190 sentences long), and yet Poe manages to develop a psychological complexity of character, setting, and action that makes the story just as intriguing today as it was almost 150 years ago.

The plot pattern of "The Cask of Amontillado" is simple, emotionally powerful, and perhaps the most popular of all time: revenge.

We've heard these tales of revenge ten thousand times. As babies we heard them in the crib as nursery rhymes; as toddlers we heard them in bed as fairy tales. We lived them in the schoolyard and saw them on television, and read them in our storybooks. Once we were grown we continued to experience the pattern throughout our lives in everything from trash novels to opera to our own personal dealing with other people: the wronged lover, the cheated business partner, the hoodwinked shopper. The revenge pattern is so old and deeply entrenched in our behavior that, in a sense, it is part of our subconscious. Even though the Bible patiently counsels us to turn the other cheek, we know a lot more about getting even.

In its simplest form, the revenge pattern supports two major characters. The first character is the Criminal, the person responsible for having committed the crime that offends the second character, the Avenger. The basic action is straightforward: the Avenger wants to get even with the Criminal.

Charles Bronson has turned the revenge pattern plot into a movie industry worth hundreds of millions of dollars in his series of *Death Wish* movies. His exploitation of the pattern is crass but powerful: first we are outraged by a series of cruel, senseless rapes and murders, and then we are delighted as the character of Charles Kersey methodically washes the streets of America of urban scum.

In "The Cask of Amontillado" Poe introduces the same basic pattern of revenge in the *very first line* of the story. "The thousand injuries of Fortunato I had borne as I best could," the narrator laments to us, "but when he ventured upon insult, I vowed revenge."

The line is remarkable for its straightforwardness and the amount of information it packs. We are told the plot pattern (revenge), the name of the criminal (Fortunato), the—albeit vague—nature of the crime (insult), and the intent of the narrator to get even. Within the first sentence (twenty-one words) the writer establishes a powerful emotional connection with the reader, and based upon the depth of the reader's experience with revenge (real and vicarious), that one line has established a series of expectations for the writer and the reader that guides the story from beginning to end.

The first line raises some basic plot questions that the reader expects to be answered (and therefore the writer must address): First, *what* did Fortunato do that was so bad that the narrator (whose name is Montresor) wants to kill him? (We want to know what Fortunato did so we can share in Montresor's outrage and again in the cleansing action of the revenge itself.) Second, *how* does Montresor plan to get even? The first question involves us in character, and the second involves us in the action/plot.

As an effective writer, you can't do more than involve your reader in both character and plot in the first line of your work. The message should be clear: involve yourself as the writer, and later your reader, in the process of expectation by raising critical questions about what's going to happen and as soon as possible in the story. Poe's first line *demands* attention, and it gives immediate force and direction to the story. As an author you are obliged to set the hook early and hard. Don't tease the reader with what *might* happen at the beginning: you may lose him. Poe's first line in "The Cask of Amontillado" demands an immediate decision of the reader: either quit (Oh, no, not another revenge story!) or continue (Oh, boy, another revenge story!). Those of us who are fans of Poe also know this won't be just another revenge story, that he'll bring something unexpected to it. This increases our anticipation even more by introducing yet other questions for us to ponder: What's the twist going to be? and When will it happen?

Imagine you're the one writing "The Cask of Amontillado" and that all you had down on paper so far was the line, "The thousand injuries of Fortunato I had borne as I best could, but when he ventured upon insult, I vowed revenge."

What will you write next?

Go ahead, try a few lines. Compare yourself with Edgar Allan Poe.

You will find, quite naturally, that the lines you write will take their cues from the first line. These cues create the "links" that join together to make a chain of events that is plot. In the first line there are three such links: a) "the thousand injuries," b) the "insult," and c) the vow of revenge. Which one did you follow up on? All of them? Or just one?

As the writer you are doing the same thing the reader does after the work is done and printed on the page: recreating the pattern. The pattern is the common denominator for both, and it doesn't make any difference if you're in the process of writing a first draft, polishing a final draft, or reading the story for the tenth time. The writer recreates the pattern by writing, and the reader recreates the pattern by reading: the pattern itself stays the same. The pattern hasn't changed since the beginning of recorded literature five thousand years ago.

The pattern is so strong it guides both the writer and the work. Remember the first line of *The Old Man and the Sea*? ("He was an old man who fished alone in a skiff in the Gulf Stream and he had gone eighty-four days now without taking a fish.") What are the "links" in that line? The entire novel (plot and all) are embedded in the first twenty-six words. Or take Tolstoy's *Anna Karenina*. That novel is a thousand pages long, and yet it starts with the same force and direction of Poe's story: "All happy families resemble one another, but each unhappy family is unhappy in its own way."

Let's go back to "The Cask of Amontillado" and compare what you wrote to what Poe actually wrote.

The first paragraph reads:

"The thousand injuries of Fortunato I had borne as I best could, but when he ventured upon insult, I vowed revenge. You, who so well know the nature of my soul, will not suppose, however, that I gave utterance to a threat. *At length* I would be avenged; this was a point definitely settled — but the very definitiveness with which it was resolved precluded the idea of risk. I must not only punish but punish with impunity. A wrong is unredressed when retribution overtakes its redresser. It is equally unredressed when the avenger fails to make himself felt as such to him who has done the wrong."

Poe does indeed connect with one of the "links" of the first line: c) the vow of revenge. These lines act as modifiers, much in the same way that adjectives modify nouns. The plot moves forward with new information (which will serve as the "links" to subsequent lines and paragraphs). We learn about Montresor from Montresor. He tells us that his revenge is a secret, that Fortunato doesn't even know it's coming; he tells us he plans to get even but not to get caught; and he tells us he plans to make Fortunato suffer.

We begin to wonder about Montresor based on this first paragraph. He seems less than honorable, for a gentleman would have the courage to confront his enemy face to face and not have to sneak behind his back. And how honorable is making your opponent suffer? We're willing to hold off judgment just yet because we still want to know the answer to our other questions: what are the "thousand injuries" and what was the "insult" that pushed Montresor over the edge?

We never do find out what Fortunato did to make Montresor so keen on killing him. That's Poe's twist. As the story progresses line by line we come to suspect Montresor is the criminal and not Fortunato, who is lured into a death trap not even aware that anything's wrong with his relationship with Montresor. The fact that the major plot questions are never answered actually makes us suspicious of Montresor and his motives because it varies from the pattern of our expectations. As readers we are saying "Before I can sympathize with you, Montresor, you have to tell me what Fortunato did." Did Fortunato have an affair with Montresor's wife? Did Fortunato slander him in public? We have no way of knowing because Poe never gives us a clue. We can't get close to Montresor because we can't share in his outrage, which we suspect now may be imagined (and Montresor may be crazy). We find ourselves put off by the cruel way Montresor exacts his revenge (he seals poor Fortunato alive in a vault without any explanation, and we know from the pattern that the avenger *always* explains to his victim why he's about to be punished). Montresor also puts us off because of the delight he gets in taunting his victim. We end up feeling less sympathy for Montresor than for Fortunato, who, like ourselves, is left to die in the dark without an explanation.

Poe took the familiar pattern of the revenge plot and reversed it, and that's the story's surprise, the element that keeps the material new and interesting. But the pattern remains the basis, the foundation from which the story is built.

The point is worth repeating: the writer recreates the pattern in the act of writing, and the reader recreates the same pattern in the act of reading. This may strike you as so obvious that it sounds stupid (the writer writes, the reader reads), but as writers we often forget that a large part of what we do is based on common experience expressed through a common language: two series of patterns that guide us from beginning to end.

This brings us back to the discussion about originality. We say we prize originality above all else in art. Originality is the artist's brilliance, that indefinable something that is distinctly the artist's and no one else's. What gets lost in all that praise of individuality is that originality is nothing more than seasoning added to stock. Seasoning gives distinct flavor, its character or charm, if you will, and seasoning gives the distinct taste that immediately identifies the dish as unique. But we forget that the foundation remains the same, and that the chef and the diner both rely on that fact.

A chef's genius is not to create a dish from original ingredients, but to combine standard ingredients in original ways. The diner recognizes the pattern established in the foundation of a baked stuffed turkey, and we look for the variation, the twist that will surprise and delight us. Perhaps it's in the glaze or in the stuffing, something that makes that turkey different from all the other turkeys that came before it.

As you develop an idea for a story, start with the foundation, the pattern of action and reaction that is plot. In *Anna Karenina*, Tolstoy even goes so far as to label one of the plot patterns in the epigraph at the beginning of the first book: "Vengeance Is Mine; I Will Repay." Then Tolstoy gives us that famous first line about unhappy families. The first links of plot are forged, and he follows through precisely according to our expectation and without delay. What unhappy family? we ask. Tolstoy tells us on the very next lines:

"Everything was upset in the Oblonskys' house. The wife had discovered an intrigue between her husband and their former French governess, and declared that she would not continue to live under the same roof with him."

More links. We recognize the pattern; the plot has begun. If you were the writer and this was all you had down on paper so far, the strength of these lines should give you direction to follow, to develop more links in the chain of events that will constitute plot. You're guided by the pattern every bit as much when you're the writer as you are when you're the reader.

THE EMPEROR'S OLD CLOTHES

I don't want to leave the impression that plot patterns are a series of abstract notions. They are very real, and they are very few. In five thousand years of recorded literature, after the creations of tens of thousands of works by men and women in hundreds of cultures, we've come up with the a sum total of thirty-six different plots.

Thirty-six, that's all.

We don't know when these thirty-six plot patterns were officially created, but they were already in place three thousand years ago with the Greeks. No one has come up with a new plot since before the birth of Christ.

It has been argued by some that the reason there have been no new plots for so long is because there are no other new intrigues to write about. The whole range of human behavior — in theory anyway — fits compactly into thirty-six categories. One explanation given as to why there are only thirty-six plots suggests there are only thirty-six human emotions, and that each plot represents one of these emotions; but I think that's a simplistic assessment of the breadth of human emotion. These plot patterns do, however, reflect our sense of how the world exists and how we exist within it. It doesn't matter if you're a Nobel laureate in literature or a hack novelist in a pulp factory: the patterns for both are exactly the same.

If thirty-six doesn't sound like many, throw in the fact that another handful of patterns — about eight — have lost their appeal to us over time because of the different way we view the world and how it works, and so they're hardly ever used anymore. Some of the patterns that were popular with the Greeks and Romans hardly ever make an appearance anymore. You might call them junkers. How many times lately have you come across a story about a man who accidentally sleeps with his mother? Or, one about a man who kills his father without realizing he's his father (maybe because he hasn't seen him since he was a baby). Both these patterns (called "Involuntary Crimes of Love" and "Kinsman Kills Unrecognized Kinsman") were popular with the Greeks and Romans (Aeschylus, Sophocles, and Seneca, for example), but today, with the world as crowded as it is, modern audiences have a lot of trouble swallowing the sheer coincidence that of all the women in the world, a man might end up with the one who turns out to be his estranged mother. (*C'mon!*) But, as always, truth is stranger than fiction. "Sixty Minutes" did a story not too long ago about a man who married a woman who turned out to be his orphaned sister — so it does happen — we just don't believe it can happen in fiction.

The story of one of the most famous fictional characters from what is arguably the most influential play in classical literature falls squarely into both of these obscure plot patterns: Oedipus both kills his father and sleeps with his mother. Sigmund Freud based a great deal of psychological theory on the pattern of *Oedipus Rex*, and for the last fifty years Freudians have been telling us every man secretly wants to sleep with his mother and every woman with her father. But even with all the psychological hoopla surrounding Oedipus (after all, it was just another Greek play for two thousand years before Freud got hold of it), very few authors have returned to that plot pattern. The French, for reasons upon which we ought not speculate, seem to give the patterns a whirl now and then (Voltaire, Corneille, and Jean Cocteau in *The Infernal Machine*), but if we could compile a list of the number of times each of the thirty-six plot patterns was used in the twentieth century, these two would certainly be at the bottom of the list.

Compare the pattern "Kinsman Kills Unrecognized Kinsman" with one of the more popular patterns, such as "Adultery" or its more exotic cousin, "Murderous Adultery." These two, as the toastmasters say, need no introduction. Everyone knows what they are and how they work. In "Adultery" Person A sleeps with Person B, and then Person A's spouse, C, finds out; a triangle with lots of variations, most of them familiar. (*Too* familiar.) In "Murderous Adultery," A sleeps with B, and then A and B try to figure out how to kill C. Remember *The Postman Always Rings Twice*? The wife and the drifter become lovers and then conspire to kill the wife's husband. Typical of the pattern. But what about the wonderful (and again typically French) twist of the pattern in the film *Diabolique* when Simone Signoret joins forces with the wife of her lover to kill her lover, who is cruel to them both. (A sleeps with B, then A and C kill B.)

We are fascinated with adultery. Modern American literature is thick with stories about it. Look at the works of John Updike, John Cheever, Ann Beattie, Judith Krantz, Jackie Collins, and Sydney Sheldon; literature, high and lowbrow alike.

Let's look at another major plot pattern: "Pursuit." In its simplest form, Person A chases Person B. Person B is often a criminal, so this pattern is typical for a lot of police and detective stories. Sherlock Holmes is in pursuit of the insidious Moriarty.

E. H. Harriman of the Union Pacific Railroad hires a posse to hunt down Butch Cassidy and the Sundance Kid.

Sometimes the person being chased isn't guilty. Cary Grant, mistaken for a CIA agent in *North by Northwest*, spends the entire film on the run. Robert Donat is pursued by police for a murder he didn't commit in another Hitchcock film, *The Thirty-Nine Steps*. Jean Valjean, guilty of stealing bread in *Les Misérables*, is relentlessly stalked by the ruthless Inspector Javert. So are the falsely accused Richard Kimble in the classic television series "The Fugitive" and David Banner in "The Incredible Hulk."

There are also many examples of the pattern in which the person is pursued by an organized force rather than by another person. Winston Smith is the victim of the repressive society of the future, Big Brother, in George Orwell's classic horror story of the future, *1984*. Likewise the main characters in *Logan's Run* and in Ray Bradbury's *Fahrenheit 451* are also hounded by their societies.

What is it about the pattern that so intrigues us? It has four dramatic elements that audiences love and therefore anticipate. These same elements, which create the pattern, also guide the author through the plot.

First, there's the *threat*. In *Butch Cassidy and the Sundance Kid*, we meet two good-natured, fun-loving outlaws who are anything but evil. They rob trains but they don't hurt people. Only E. H. Harriman of the Union Pacific doesn't take to having his trains robbed.

So Harriman hires a private posse to kill Butch and Sundance, who, of course, run for cover, thus reaching the second dramatic phase, *flight*.

Butch and Sundance take off with Harriman's hit men hot on their heels, and so begins *the chase*, the third phase. Butch and Sundance are clever and do everything they can to lose the men gunning for them, but the men chasing them are always just one step behind them whatever they do. "Hey, Butch," Sundance shouts at his partner from a full gallop.

"What?" demands Cassidy, his mind on escape, not conversation.

"They're very good," Sundance admits the obvious.

So good in fact they chase the pair out of the country to Bolivia where they resume their careers as robbers.

Threat leads to the second dramatic phase of the pattern of "Pursuit" —*flight*, which leads to the third phase —*the chase*, which in turn must resolve itself in the fourth and final phase of the pattern —*capture*. *Capture* may be temporary (true master criminals like Moriarty somehow always manage to give their pursuers the slip at the last moment), or it may be permanent. (Butch and Sundance are gunned down by the Bolivian army in a last stand.)

The point of the final phase is to resolve the issues of the story and plot, which are brought together into sharp focus in the climax. During capture anything can happen, depending upon the author's seasoning of the pattern, from straightforward solutions (the innocent go free, the guilty are punished) to full ironic reversal (the innocent are punished, and the guilty go free).

Obviously space won't allow for me to cover the other thirty plot patterns. However, I've included a list and short description of each with some examples at the end of the book for reference.

Don't underestimate the importance these plot patterns play in the development of your work. They are the foundations upon which all literature is built. Everything within your story, from characterization to dialogue to story depends upon the creation of a strong foundation. If it is weak, if it is incomplete or confused, then your work will eventually collapse.

The cause of most failed writing is not that the writer's ideas are bad, but that the author either presents an incomplete or confused pattern or fails to season the pattern sufficiently to make it interesting.

The pattern is your guide. Don't make the mistake of relying entirely on intuition and hoping things work out for the best. Shooting from the hip is an invitation to disaster. Writing is a combination of both method and madness, and no one can say in what proportion. The relationship between the two is probably in line with Thomas Edison's summary of genius as 10% inspiration (madness) and 90% perspiration (method).

Madness is the seasoning. It is unique and indefinable. Method is what this book is about.

DEATH IN THE WOODS

The following guidelines will help clarify and simplify the task of creating a plot and adapting a pattern.

1. *Study the pattern that best suits your story.* Review the patterns in this chapter and at the back of the book and decide which one (or ones, since they may overlap) best suits your idea. If you don't find a pattern that matches your idea, don't celebrate the discovery of the first new plot pattern in three thousand years just yet. It may be that either your idea is too vague, in which case it may not seem to fit anywhere, or you've overlooked the pattern that does apply.

When you identify the pattern or patterns that do apply, study examples of the pattern and then,

2. *Determine what the dramatic phases of the pattern are.* In "Pursuit" there were four phases: threat, flight, the chase, and capture. There are usually three or four dramatic phases in any given pattern.

Let's say you decided to write a story about a young boy named Jonathan who accidentally kills his older brother, Michael, in a hunting accident.

Which of the thirty-six patterns would this story suit?

Obviously "Adultery" and "Murderous Adultery" are out. So are "Revolt," "Pursuit," "Daring Enterprise," and "Obtaining." What about "Fatal Imprudence"? After all, Jonathan was careless, and his carelessness cost Michael his life.

"Fatal Imprudence" looks good at first, but the pattern of "Fatal Imprudence" doesn't fit this story. In this pattern, Person A is told (or warned) not to do something and then goes ahead and does it anyway. (Dramatic phases: 1. Prohibition, 2. Temptation, 3. Disobedience, 4. Resolution/Punishment) The focus of the pattern is wrong for the story. You want to concentrate on the emotional impact of the accident on Jonathan, whereas "Fatal Imprudence" is really about what happens when curiosity overwhelms fear of dire consequences. (Fairy tales contain perfect examples of these plot patterns. For an example of "Fatal Imprudence" read Grimm's Bluebeard story, "Fitcher's Bird.")

All right, then, what about "Remorse" as a pattern?

Remorse: a gnawing distress arising from a sense of guilt for past wrongs. Looks promising as a pattern, but is it the right one?

That depends upon the focus you bring to the story. If you plan to concentrate on Jonathan's feelings of guilt and remorse, and how this tragic event affects him as a kind of psychological study of despair, then the focus of the plot is the character of Jonathan. If this is the case, then the subject of the plot is "Remorse."

What are the dramatic phases of the pattern?

At first Jonathan may deny he was responsible for shooting Michael. He insists someone else did it, not he, even though it's obvious to everyone else Jonathan was responsible. Jonathan feels isolated, alone, separated from his family and friends, even the world.

Then Jonathan begins to realize what he at first refused to acknowledge, that he did shoot his brother. Denial turns into anger. Perhaps Jonathan is angry at Michael for being careless. ("He should've known better," Jonathan rationalizes in order to protect himself from the truth. "He shouldn't have gone off by himself.")

Jonathan hasn't reached his despair yet because of the first dramatic phase in which he avoids dealing with the pain and guilt that ultimately must come (in a later phase).

The second dramatic phase of this pattern would start with Jonathan's struggle with the truth. He accepts responsibility for his brother's death, and it devastates him. Numbness or stoicism are replaced with a sense of great loss. Family and friends try to cheer him, but to no avail. Jonathan sinks lower and lower into his depression. He can't eat, he can't sleep, he becomes unbearable to the people around him. He is a wreck, and his life is going down the tubes.

Finally, at his lowest point, something happens or someone comes along to help Jonathan climb out of his hole. Perhaps he saves another person's life. Perhaps he falls in love and his girlfriend gently guides him back among the living. Any number of things can happen, but the point of the dramatic phase is that Jonathan must come to terms with himself and killing his brother (if the story is to have an upbeat ending) or he must at least try and perhaps fail (if the story is to have a downbeat ending). In either case, Jonathan reaches the final phase of dramatic development in the pattern—acceptance—in which he must deal with what has happened to his brother and to himself and learn to put the tragedy behind him as best he can (or fail trying).

The "Remorse" pattern works *if* the focus you wish to bring to the story deals with Jonathan learning to deal with the demons inside himself. But suppose you have a different focus in mind?

Suppose you are more concerned with the effect of the tragedy on the entire family, not just Jonathan, and you want to show how an event such as this could devastate everyone, not just Jonathan. The first pattern concentrates on Jonathan's feelings and so takes his point of view. But suppose you want to concentrate on the family itself, not just one member in it. Then "Remorse" won't work as a pattern anymore.

What then?

"Loss of a Loved One"? This pattern may look good at first glance but again the dramatic pattern is wrong for what you want to accomplish. This pattern doesn't allow for the witness of the "crime" to be the one who committed it. The pattern would work if Jonathan had witnessed his brother's death, but not if Jonathan himself was responsible for that death.

Then let's try one of the plot patterns that is no longer so popular, "Kinsman Kills Unrecognized Kinsman."

The obvious first dramatic phase of the pattern is the event/"crime" itself in which Jonathan shoots and kills Michael. Now, instead of concentrating on Jonathan and his feelings, we concentrate on how Michael's death affects the family. (In ways this approach is similar to *Ordinary People* with Donald Sutherland,

Mary Tyler Moore, and Timothy Hutton, in which the family must deal with a son's sudden accidental death.) Let's say the father cannot forgive Jonathan, and he becomes angry and bitter and rejects Jonathan. Or perhaps the mother, stricken with sorrow, turns to the bottle. I don't want to make the story sound too melodramatic, but the point I want to make is that the focus of the story is on the complex and powerful emotional dynamic that is taking place inside the *family* and not just inside one person.

The family must struggle with the same feelings of anger, denial, depression, and acceptance as Jonathan did in the dramatic phases of "Remorse." The question isn't so much whether Jonathan can overcome these destructive feelings, but whether the family itself can survive the tragedy. The dramatic thrust is the same, but the focus is different. So "Kinsman Kills Unrecognized Kinsman" would indeed work as a possible plot pattern.

The point to make clear is that in choosing a plot pattern you have to make certain decisions about your story and how you intend to tell it. In the case of Jonathan and Michael, you had to choose whether the story is just about Jonathan's internal struggle with guilt ("Remorse") or is it about a family that is ravaged by an accident ("Kinsman Kills Unrecognized Kinsman"). The patterns themselves are flexible and can adapt themselves to a variety of people and situations. But choose one that suggests a pattern of action that is consistent with what you have in mind for the story you want to tell.

Once you feel comfortable with the pattern that best suits your idea,

3. *Translate each dramatic phase of the pattern into action.* Pick up with the first dramatic phase of the pattern and figure out how you can accomplish in one line what Poe, Tolstoy, and Hemingway accomplished in the examples I've quoted. Whether you're writing a short-short story, a thousand-page novel, or a movie of the week makes no difference. A fast start is essential both to the writer and to the reader.

In the example we're using of Jonathan and Michael (let's say we've decided to use "Kinsman Kills Unrecognized Kinsman" as the plot pattern), we have to decide how best to start the story.

You could start the story the morning of the accident before dawn at the family breakfast table. You could introduce each of the family members—the mother making breakfast for her two boys, the father giving advice about where to find deer, Jonathan's excitement about going out with his older brother, and Michael, still half-asleep and half put-off that he has to take his little brother with him.

This scene has several values. It establishes the main characters so we can see what they're like and how they relate to each other *before* the tragedy so we can later understand (by contrast) how much they've changed under stress.

The problem with this start, however, is that it's anything but a fast start. Nothing happening. No tension. Important character development, yes, but the writing will lack the punch of the first line that propels both writer and reader forward as in the examples above.

You could begin the story later, say once the boys were already in the woods and on the hunt. We could meet Michael (our last chance to know him before he dies), and we could learn about the nature of the relationship between the brothers (are they competitive, adulatory, resentful, what?). As with the scene in the family kitchen, we learn valuable information about the characters before the critical action begins.

But we still have the same problem: a slow start. Neither beginning moves us into the first dramatic phase of the pattern. So then, how to begin?

4. *Begin the scene as late as possible.* Don't enter a scene in a leisurely way and slowly build toward the main action of the scene. Start at the point where the actual critical action begins. In this case you might begin the story of Jonathan and Michael with a line like: "As Jonathan slowly squeezed the trigger, he was filled with a dark sense of foreboding." We know immediately something is wrong. The "links" in the chain of cause and effect are forged. The story begins immediately. As a writer you should know how to proceed from this point.

But this approach presents a problem too. We lose the advantage of knowing the main characters (the father, the mother, Michael, and Jonathan) before the critical event. How do we compare the characters if we don't know who they are to begin with?

By combining both approaches. Flashbacks are one of fiction's greatest assets. A writer must learn to manipulate time. You must learn how to present the story in a time sequence that keeps the pattern on track (in its dramatic phases), that maintains tension, and still teaches us what we need to know about people, places, and events. You could start the story at the moment Jonathan pulls the trigger on his brother and then interweave flashbacks of the family that morning at the breakfast table, and even later with the two brothers in the woods before the hunt actually begins. This way you achieve a balance between the slower, expository writing (background) and the faster paced writing of the action in the present.

Of all the discussions of pattern in this book, this one is the most critical. Over the years I've seen many writers launch into projects blindly, with only a vague sense of the story they want to write. This approach is something like going fishing without a pole, holding out your hands and hoping a fish will jump into them. It can happen, but it's not likely. The main point I want to make is that you have to take the responsibility for developing plot into your own hands, and when you're sitting at a table and your mind is drawing a complete blank, there is a way you can chart your story in order to give you direction.

No good house was ever made without a blueprint.

CHAPTER 5

PATTERN IN ACTION

Action is eloquence

William Shakespeare,
Coriolanus 3:2

WE THREE KINGS

When the Egyptian architects of the pharaohs first proposed the concept of the true pyramid, everyone must have thought they'd spent too much time out in the sun. Pick out a place in the middle of the desert with nothing around but sand, sand, sand, and assemble a gigantic triangle made of almost two-and-a-half-million blocks of stone weighing an average of 2 ½ tons apiece.

The ruler of the Upper and Lower Kingdoms must have been perplexed. Why? he no doubt demanded.

It'll be the greatest monument ever built to a man, argued the chief architect, who was certainly the greatest salesman of his day. A monument that will never perish; one that will stand for all time.

The idea obviously appealed to the pharaoh—perhaps it was his administration's answer to seasonal unemployment by putting 100,000 able-bodied men to work for twenty years.

And now, almost four thousand years later, the pyramids outside Cairo in Giza still stand with the same sense of solidity and timelessness as when they were built.

In a pinch most of us couldn't say to save our lives whose pyramids they were. What were the names of the great kings who were buried there? At least when we visit Grant's tomb we have an idea who's buried there.

Maybe nobody except diehard Egyptologists, whose job it is to know, really cares who was buried in the pyramids. The names are unimportant. What's important are the pyramids themselves; they are one of the seven wonders of the world.

One truth is evident, however. The pyramids represent the skillful culmination of power and intellect. They are architectural and aesthetic genius. Even today they do not fail to awe and make you wonder how on earth it was ever done.

The point of this cautionary tale is to divorce *you* from *your work*. Like the pharaohs, we sometimes get caught up in the ego of the thing. (I'm a writer, this is my work.) We have a hard time looking at the thing objectively. We get caught up in the events and the emotions of the story and sometimes fail to see what army-types are fond of calling The Big Picture.

None of the pyramids could've been built without a painstakingly detailed Big Picture. Part of the beauty of the pyramids was its creators' ability to fuse into a single, three-dimensional shape, simultaneous patterns of structure (the pyramid itself), of thought (the religious and political symbolism), of character (the great king in his chamber surrounded not only by his possessions to accompany him to the next world, but a historical testament of his deeds and what it meant to be an Egyptian king), and exquisite patterns of time, place, and language. Each of the separate elements works in harmony with each of the other elements.

Actions are blocks similar to the stone hewn by the quarrymen for the pyramids. Each has its own specific weight, function, and position in the pattern of plot (which is the architect's blueprint). It has its own momentum as it moves into position.

When the great pyramids at Giza were being built, no one said, all right, fellas, cut a bunch of stones and then haul them out into the desert so we can try to figure out how to put them together. Think for a moment of the mathematical complexity and engineering savvy that went into building a pyramid. The exterior stones of the pyramid aren't made of squares (that would be too easy) or of triangles (that would be just as easy) but precise rhomboids calculated for complex variables such as pitch, angle, stress, and so forth. The architects had to know exactly what they wanted before it was made. *Their action depended upon concept.* A pyramid is made of precise angles. So is a well-wrought story.

By the way, the three Egyptian kings who were buried in the pyramids at Giza were Khufu, Khafre, and Menkaure. Ring any bells?

A GHOST STORY

Once you've decided upon a master plan, a blueprint, a plot pattern — whatever name you want to call it — you now need to translate the concept, the idea that started you out, into action. Events. Who does what, when. We already defined action as the course of events within the story, but with the addition that events are not enough in themselves, no more than stones are enough to build a pyramid. The stones, the events of the story, have to be calculated, crafted to fit the structural pattern, so that when you stand back and look at your work, you don't see individual stones, you see a whole — each stone meshed so tightly with its neighbor that it appears seamless to the eye. You can accomplish this only by carrying out your plan from the large conceptual level of structure and plot, to the midlevel range of action (and in the next chapter, character), to the fine-tuning of language and symbolism. (Think of your progress as a writer as pyramidal: the base of the pyramid represents structure and plot; the midsection represents character and action, and the peak of the pyramid represents language and symbolism: each level builds on the level preceding it, each successive level more refined in its thinking and doing.)

A common mistake of many beginning writers is to think of action as nothing more than a series of successive events, like beads on a string. First this happens, then that happens, and so forth. But action is responsible for building tension, for gaining momentum in a story. And to do that, you have to learn how to pace action so that events build dramatically. *This* happens and causes *that* to happen, suddenly. Events should have a rhythm, and they should rely on each other for their dramatic impact. An excellent example of rhythm in action is Oliver Stone's film, *Platoon*. The film starts out with Taylor arriving in Vietnam. The scene is tense but calm. The very next scene Taylor is on patrol in the bush, experiencing the terrors of being a "new guy": he sees his first corpse, he is attacked by ferocious jungle ants. The second scene turns up the tension of the first scene by making Taylor's premonition of disaster start to become real. But the horrors he experiences in the second scene are nothing compared to what he is about to experience: the death of a comrade. Each scene in the film builds on the tension of the previous scenes. Each horror becomes more horrific. Just as Taylor believes he is adjusting to the nightmare of Vietnam, he is thrust into the ultimate horrors of war. Stone's screenplay builds toward the apocalyptic final scene, and every scene along the way makes a small contribution to that end.

I'm going to try a bit of heresy here. Instead of giving an example from fiction to illustrate my point, I'm going to resort to poetry instead. You might object at first, saying poetry and fiction are different things and don't share that much technique, but that just ain't so. The two have a lot in common, especially narrative poetry, which is in the same business as short-story writing and novel and screenwriting: telling a story.

The poem is by Robert Frost. Not too many people know "The Witch of Coos," but it's one of his best.

The story is presented simply. A traveler, unnamed, spends the night for shelter with an old woman and her son. The traveler listens; in fact, he never speaks. The old woman, who claims indirectly to be a witch, and her son tell a tale of adultery, murder, and revenge. (Sound familiar?) The plot pattern contains elements of murderous adultery and revenge. See if you can determine which pattern is the correct one for the story as it is told.

The Mother is sewing while she tells her tale. She has her

sewing basket by her side and from time to time throughout the poem stops to look for a particular button.

The Son, who is a kind of chorus for the mother, claims she can make a table rear and kick like an army mule.

The Mother pooh-poohs such parlor tricks. She would rather talk about the dead and asks the traveler if he doesn't think the dead have something they're holding back.

The Son, as if on cue, asks the Mother if she wouldn't rather tell the traveler what secret they have hidden in the attic.

She answers him simply: "Bones," she says, "a skeleton."

The Son then tells the traveler his mother's bed is pushed up against the door to the attic to keep the bones from getting out. "Mother hears it in the night," he claims, "halting perplexed behind the barrier of door and headboard." The bones, he says, want to get back into the cellar where they came from.

But the mother insists with a touch of glee that they'll never let the bones out of the attic.

Note how Frost doesn't warm up to the story but jump starts it. We learn very quickly that there's a skeleton trapped in the house that wants to get into the cellar, and that for some yet undisclosed reason, the Mother and Son have trapped it in the attic. Immediate plot questions arise. Whose are the bones? Why do they want to get out of the attic? How did they get there in the first place? As readers we expect to get the answers, and as writers, we must address the same questions in the translation of plot to action.

The Son continues to tell the tale. The skeleton left the cellar forty years ago, carrying itself up the stairs into the kitchen and then upstairs to the bedroom. The Son confesses he was a baby and doesn't know where he was at the time.

The Mother picks up the story. She was downstairs alone when she heard someone coming up the stairs from the cellar one step at a time, ominously, slowly. She knew it wasn't her husband; he was upstairs in bed. Who then? It was the bones, she says.

Unable to contain her curiosity, she opens the door to the cellar, only to find the bones coming at her, fingers outstretched, "the way he did in life once." The Mother slaps off the hand of the skeleton and the finger-pieces scatter across the kitchen floor. (At this point the Mother searches her button box for one of the finger bones.)

The skeleton, rebuffed, heads upstairs for the bedroom. The Mother yells to warn her husband to shut the door. But Toffile (the husband) doesn't understand and thinks company has come. He doesn't want to get out of his warm bed.

The Mother rushes up the stairs and into the dark bedroom. It's in the room, she tells her startled husband. The bones!

What bones? he demands.

The ones from the cellar, she explains. The ones from the grave.

Toffile sprints out of bed and together the pair try to mow down the skeleton by swinging their arms at knee level. Then they decide to try to trap the bones with an open door to the attic. The trick works and they nail the door shut.

Every night the bones come down the stairs and stand perplexed behind the door, trying to figure out how to get past the door into the bedroom. The Mother then admits that she had promised to be cruel to the bones, because they had once been cruel to her husband.

We learn then that Toffile had killed a man and buried him in the cellar. The Mother says he was a man Toffile killed *instead* of killing her.

The Mother ends her story by insisting she's telling the truth, all the while looking for the finger-bone in her button box.

The traveler, upon leaving the next morning, confirms the name on his way out: Toffile Lajway.

Of course the telling loses force and detail in my retelling, but you get the general idea. I've only highlighted the important material; Frost spins a bona fide New England yarn.

On first reading, the story seems pretty straightforward as a tale of the supernatural. As I pointed out, the plot questions are raised early (Whose are the bones? Why do they want to get out of the cellar? How did they get there in the first place?) and each of the questions, in turn, gets answered. The skeleton belongs to a man Toffile killed and buried in the cellar. We pick up from several important clues that the man was the Mother's illicit lover. (Remember when she slaps the hand of the bones as he comes at her with his hand outstretched *"the way he did in life once"*? Remember when the Mother tells the traveler that her husband killed the man *instead* of her?) A triangle. Adultery that turns into murder. Pattern: A (the man) makes love to B (the Mother); C (the husband) finds out and kills A.

The plot pattern is Murderous Adultery, right?

Not really.

Notice the focus of the story is on the telling of the story by the Mother and the Son. The Son doesn't say that much, and from one very important detail, we can discount what he says about his mother. Here is a forty-year-old man who sounds very much like a child and still lives with his mother. (We know his age from his speech when he says it happened forty years ago when he was a baby.)

In fact, when you go back and look at the details of the story carefully, you will see a very different pattern emerge. Beneath the surface of this ghost story lies another horror story, one which is more subtle and psychologically complex. We, like the traveler, have sat through the telling of the tale without saying anything. The story of murder and walking skeletons has entertained us. The Mother's whimsical descriptions make us smile, and maybe for a moment or two, while she was talking about the murder (*Toffile's* revenge) we even shiver a bit. But for the person who looks at the teller as well as the tale, the focus of the story changes.

For the reader sensitive to inconsistencies (which are the essence of clues in a mystery), small but telling details give away a different story that is every much as horrifying as the one the Mother herself tells. It's hard not to be taken in by the Mother's story because it's so colorful and macabre. But Frost seems to be saying "look deeper" and see what lies deep beneath the surface of the tale.

A few of the clues I've already mentioned. The Son, who *sounds* like he might be eight or ten years old, turns out to be forty and therefore probably a bit simple. He isn't a reliable witness. In fact if you look at what he says, you realize he's neither seen nor heard the bones himself. They've been trapped in the attic since he was a baby. He isn't a witness; he is merely his mother's straight man. Of course he believes there are bones in the attic. His mother hears them in the night, he tells the traveler. But he himself hasn't heard anything.

Toffile, of course, is dead, so we can't learn anything from him. Scratch another witness. But from the Mother's telling of the tale, we realize that even while he was alive, Toffile hadn't heard or seen any bones either.

Only the Mother has.

A pattern of behavior is emerging. Can we trust the story she's been telling us?

Like all ghost stories, it depends upon whether you *want* to believe the Mother. Skeptics will suspect the teller before they buy into such an outrageous tale; true believers will accept the tale outright. Both are horror stories. The one story simply lies hidden beneath the other.

We do know, from the Mother's own admission, that she is overwhelmed with guilt for her affair with the dead man and for her husband's murder of him. Beneath this guilt, however, she still longs for her lover, and during the tale she remembers him fondly. With her husband now dead and her life being alone with her simple son, that longing continued to grow with time. Note that the skeleton comes down the stairs from the attic and stands behind the headboard of the Mother's *bed*. A revealing detail. But she has promised her husband to be cruel to the bones. Why? Because she and the bones had once done something that was cruel to her husband.

The plot pattern is "Remorse." (Remember this pattern from the previous chapter?) At this deeper, psychological level, the story is about a woman and her deep-seated feelings of guilt. The focus is the Mother, not the story she tells. How does Robert Frost translate this pattern into specific action?

The poet had a clear idea of what he wanted to accomplish in "The Witch of Coos" (his idea), and used the pattern of plot ("Revenge") in order to accomplish it. The pattern of action in the story creates the effect he wanted to achieve. Let's go back and see how Frost accomplished this.

First he introduces the traveler, who is kept vague and silent so that we may identify with him (or her). The Mother and Son did all the talking, says the traveler. Why? To do anything else would distract from the real story. The traveler is everyman. He has no face.

The Mother begins the first speech. All the speeches in the poem are presented in the same fashion as in a play. The Mother's speeches are preceded by MOTHER and the Son's speeches are identified by SON. Point? The point is that the traveler shouldn't interfere with the story. The point is to have the tale come *directly* from the Mother, without having to be retold by the traveler. If the traveler told us what the Mother said, then we might suspect the traveler, which needlessly complicates the story and contradicts the "idea." Remember, the focus of the story is the Mother, not the traveler. This is an excellent example of concept translated into action.

Second is the ploy of the button. The Mother starts and finishes the poem looking for a button, which she never finds. The button, you'll remember, is one of the finger bones of the skeleton that she got when she slapped off its hand when it first came up from the cellar.

The finger bone is the only tangible proof we have that any of this ever really happened. But the Mother can't come up with the proof, and we leave her at the end of the poem still looking for it. Again, concept translated into action.

Third, as I've pointed out, the quick start raises some hard plot questions, and these three questions direct the action of the story.

The first plot question is "Whose are the bones?" The poem is, like any fiction, a mystery, and in mysteries, you don't want to give solutions away easily or too early. So Frost describes the journey of the bones out of the cellar, past the Mother, who slaps off its hand, and upstairs to the bedroom and ultimately to the attic. During the course of this journey, we get some important additional clues to keep the plot question alive. "It was the bones," says the Mother. "I knew them—and good reason." How did she know them? we ask ourselves. And what was the good reason?

The most revealing action during the journey of the bones that starts to answer our question is when the skeleton reaches out to touch the Mother. "Then he came at me with one hand outstretched, the way he did in life once; but this time I struck the hand off brittle on the floor." These lines not only answer our question about whose the bones are, but also how the Mother happens to know them — with good reason.

As the Mother continues her story (or should we call it a confession?), she answers the third plot question: "How did the bones get into the cellar?" Toffile murdered his wife's lover and buried his bones there, that's how.

But it's the second plot question that holds the "answer" to the mystery. Why do the bones want to get out of the cellar? That plot question doesn't get the direct answer that the other two got. Why after forty years did the bones get out of the grave, march up the cellar stairs, and then go upstairs to the bedroom?

This question is answered, but it is answered much more subtly, and it is answered with clues along the way rather than with a definitive answer as in the case of the other two plot questions. The answer is woven into the details of the story. The bones have been resurrected in the imagination of the Mother who has been living with the guilt of her affair and the knowledge that her murdered lover was buried beneath her feet in the cellar. Imagination compounded by time. Guilt compounded by desire and the yearning for her lost lover. This detail, perhaps more than any other, raises "The Witch of Coos" above just another ghost story to that of psychological thriller. It is the seasoning of the stock.

Without the answer to the second plot question, the story fails to make any real sense. We may get taken in by the details of the event and Frost's colorful writing, but the real issue is this second question. We need to know the answers to the other questions in order to understand the final question, but the pieces come together and unify into a whole. There is nothing that happens in this story that doesn't contribute in some significant way to the answering of the plot questions.

The pattern of action in a story, then, must dedicate itself directly (as in the case of plot questions one and three) and indirectly (as in the case of plot question two) to the answering of the plot questions raised at the beginning of the story.

Here are some specific guidelines for you to consider, when writing your own story, on how to develop a pattern of action.

1. After you've written a scene, ask yourself in what way (or ways) did the scene contribute to developing or answering (in part or in whole, directly or indirectly) the plot questions you have raised.

2. When you're stuck and don't know how to proceed, ask yourself what the plot questions are in your story and how you may direct your effort toward answering them.

3. Do not overwhelm the reader with plot questions. Usually two or three are enough. If you overcomplicate matters, then you'll find yourself side-tracking in order to answer all the questions. Notice how tightly bound the three plot questions of "The Witch of Coos" are, and how the total energy of the story goes into answering them.

4. Don't delay giving answers. Some answers you can give early (such as the question, "Whose are the bones?") and some answers must come slowly and over time (such as "Why do the bones want to get out of the cellar?"). Pace the answers from beginning to end. Don't give away too much too soon, but then don't hold back too long, because it will frustrate and eventually alienate the reader. The reader must feel that he or she is making progress with the mystery, and so you must give answers, and parts of answers, along the way to satisfy him or her.

5. Make certain that the action is consistent with the dramatic phases of the pattern. The pattern, the dramatic phases of the pattern, and the action combine to make the foundation of your pyramid. The three must work together, each consistent with the others.

If you follow these suggestions on how to develop action from the pattern of plot, not only will you spend less time pulling out your hair, but you will find your story developing more aggressively. Ideas will come more freely, and you'll have a greater sense of what you should—and should not—include in the story. Actions are the links in the chain of cause and effect, and the plot pattern is your guide to creating action.

Action is the means; plot is its end.

CHAPTER 6

PATTERN IN CHARACTER

MOMMY AND DADDY
AND BABY MAKE THREE

Action is character; character is action. You've heard it before.
You are what you do. So the link between plot and character
through action is inevitable. Plot is action, and character is action. This chapter isn't about creating characters, but rather how
to develop a pattern of behavior (character) that is consistent
with the pattern of action (plot). This is the middle section of
the pyramid I talked about in the last chapter.

As you embark on your story and bring each of the major
characters into play, you enter the realm of character dynamics.
Character dynamics deal with how each character relates to each
of the other major characters in the plot.

Let's start with a character dynamic of one. A single major
character. Protagonist but no antagonist. Is there such a story?
No, there isn't. You might say what about man against himself
or man against the mountain, for example? The nature of fiction
is conflict: someone *against* someone or something else. For that
to happen, there have to be at least two people (or one person
and a force). The someone might be a person himself, as in a
person who is fighting the forces of good and evil within himself,
and the something might be anything inanimate, but the point
is that there is a struggle going on between forces, whether those
forces be internal (as in the case of a person struggling within

79

himself) or external (as in the case of a person struggling against the forces of nature).

Let's try a character dynamic of two then. The interaction between the two elements is simple. The dynamic has a factor of two: A relates to B, and B relates to A. Poe's "The Cask of Amontillado" has only two characters: Montresor and Fortunato. We see how the two interact with one another and draw our conclusions on the basis of what they say and do. The dynamic of two is much more common to short stories than to longer works such as screenplays or novels. The reason is practical: space. Short stories are concentrated experiences in time and place, whereas longer works have the room to explore human relationships much more deeply. Several of Hemingway's short stories concentrate on one-to-one character relationships, as in "Cat in the Rain," "Old Man at the Bridge," "Mr. and Mrs. Elliot," and the famous "Hills Like White Elephants."

The most common character dynamic, however, has three major characters. This dynamic has a factor of six. (Notice how the factor increases geometrically rather than arithmetically: two characters have a factor of two; three characters have a factor of six; four characters have a factor of twelve.) Welcome to the home of the classic triangle. We have three major characters: A, B, and C. The story will examine how A relates to B and to C; how B relates to A and to C; and how C relates to A and to B — a total of six relationships.

This may sound confusing but actually it's the most common of all the dynamics and also the most comfortable for both reader and writer. In *2001: A Space Odyssey*, the author takes three character elements (two men and a computer named HAL), isolates them in a spaceship on a long journey, and then examines what happens when the computer, capable of artificial intelligence, begins to develop some negative characteristics of human personality such as suspicion and paranoia.

Even a story with as many different characters as *M*A*S*H* has three major characters at its core: protagonists Hawkeye Pierce (played by Donald Sutherland in the film), Trapper John (played by Eliot Gould), and antagonist Frank Burns (played by, believe it or not, Robert Duvall). The character dynamic of three is so basic to most fiction that any list of such works would be endless, whether it be in serious films such as Francois Truffaut's *Jules and Jim* or any of George Lucas' films in the *Star Wars* trilogy (Luke Skywalker and Obi-Wan Kenobi and Darth Vader in the primary plot triangle, and Han Solo, Chewbacca, and Princess Leia in the secondary triangle). In *Return of the Jedi*, in the triangle of Luke, Darth Vader, and the Emperor, the struggle for control see-saws constantly among the three characters, creating a masterful tension that doesn't relent until the final resolution. Every major western made in Hollywood since *Fort Apache* (which has three triangles in it) and *Shane* (which has only one) has used the triangle.

In fact, it's difficult not to have a triangle in many of the plot patterns. The obvious patterns are "Adultery" and "Murderous Adultery" which demand a cast of three. Over half the plot patterns require a triangle in order to happen at all, so when you choose which plot pattern applies to the story you want to write, make sure you understand the basic nature of the character dynamic that goes along with it.

If you try to increase the character dynamic from three to four, your troubles will start. The dynamic is now twelve — twelve relationships to worry about among four characters. Clearly this is a major burden for the writer and even a burden for the reader who must try to keep track of the myriad relationships between people. Skillful writers are capable of pulling off such a feat, but it's a full-time job balancing so many interactions.

The rule of thumb is two characters is too few (except in short stories) and four characters is too many. Three is just right. Three is balance; neither oversimplified nor overcomplicated. Three's definitely not a crowd here.

Three Times Three

The triangle is the basis for human relations in most fiction. But fiction doesn't have to be limited to a single triangle of relationships. Depending on the complexity of your work, you may include any number of lesser or greater triangles in it. You may, for instance, include a major triangle of relationships among major characters and then a minor triangle of relationships among minor characters in your subplot. Dickens routinely developed series of lesser triangular relationships in his novels. An excellent example worth reading is *David Copperfield*. Copperfield has relationships with a series of people, from the unforgettable Mr. Micawber to the evil Uriah Heep, to the two women who love him, Dora Spenlow and Agnes Wickfield. David Copperfield's relationships with all sections of society put him in triangle after triangle as the novel exposes the inhuman treatment of children in nineteenth-century England. Dickens was so careful in his construction of character triangles that they permeated even the simplest level of action. In the Peggoty family, for instance, Little Em'ly Peggoty, who is engaged to Ham Peggoty (a distant cousin), falls under the trance of Steerforth, who seduces her and then leads her astray. In an ironic twist, Ham Peggoty dies trying to rescue Steerforth from a shipwreck.

The important rule to remember when developing triangles in your work is that the triangles should not compete with each other. Develop them in a hierarchy of importance. The major characters have their triangle; the minor characters have theirs. One major character, such as the central character of your work, may participate in more than one triangle, but you should avoid confusing the reader with too many relationships, especially if they are of equal importance. The Russian novelists were very good at this sort of complication, but then their works often ran to a thousand pages. Shakespeare often limited his triangles to three: one major and two minors. And according to the rule of three, that's the perfect balance.

ARMCHAIR PSYCHIATRY I

Now that you've matched the right number of major characters with your plot pattern, the next step is to develop a pattern of behavior for each of the characters. You want to develop your characters so they're not just functions of plot, because if that's all they are, then the story will seem flat and artificial. The people need to come to life, and for them to come to life, they have to be convincing.

How do you create a convincing character?

By his pattern of behavior.

Oftentimes we create characters who simply enter a scene, say a few words, do a thing or two, and then move on to the next scene, one after the other, until they reach the end of the work. These characters don't touch us because they are being used only as devices to make the plot work. When the story itself becomes more important than the people in the story, then the work is hollow because it lacks the humanity of full characterization. The characters are puppets, no more.

As much as everyone likes O. Henry's famous story, "The Gift of the Magi," the emphasis of the story isn't upon the people and their sacrifices for each other for the sake of love, but upon the gimmick of ironical reversal. The author concentrates not on feelings, but on events, and so when the man trades in his gold watch to buy his sweetheart an ivory comb for her hair, and when the woman cuts off her long hair to sell to buy a gold fob for her sweetheart's watch, each has made a great sacrifice only to be left with a useless gift. But O. Henry didn't delve into people as real people, he cared only for the event itself. The people serve no other purpose than to make the plot happen. The characters are one-dimensional, flat, and nondescript. This may be all right for a short-short story which doesn't place such a high premium on characterization, but in longer works such as novels and screenplays, we demand fuller treatment of characters.

In our own personal lives we recognize people not only from their physical appearance, but also by their behavior. If your next-door neighbor were sitting stark naked in a lawn chair out on the front lawn of his house waving to cars as they drove by, you would probably think his actions were out of character (unless, of course, your neighbor does this on a regular basis). You would be alarmed, and would either try to talk your neighbor back into his house or call the men in the white coats.

From our knowledge of people, we expect them to act in certain ways based upon how they've acted in the past, and any radical departure from this pattern of behavior alerts us to trouble. If a teetotaling aunt suddenly expressed a strong taste for Irish whiskey, we would automatically wonder what happened to Auntie Ethel to give her a taste for the jug. As witnesses to the behavior of others, we tend to project behavior based upon past performance, and when a person doesn't conform to our expectations, we wonder what happened.

We form relationships with people based upon their behavior; we conduct business with people based upon their behavior; everywhere we go and everything we do involves a constant evaluation of other people's behavior. We are all analysts when it comes to other people. Some people are better at it than others, and draw better conclusions about people based upon what they observe. Others of us are hopeless because we interpret everything wrong. But the point is, whether we're good or bad at "reading" other people's behavior, we all do it constantly. From our family members to strangers on the street, we're always looking, analyzing, and comparing notes against what we might call a standard of conduct for each person.

The same ideas hold true for creating characters in fiction. The reader continues to make the same types of observations about characters on the page as the characters he sees on the street. The reader compares the actions of fictional characters with his knowledge of the actions of real people. You have to invest your major characters with a significant range of behavior to allow that kind of evaluation by the reader.

This does *not* mean a character should be predictable. Predictable means boring. Fiction is about change in character, change that occurs as the result of stress. And it's stress that often pushes characters into areas of behavior where they might never have been before. A character is not capable of all kinds of action, but only those acts that are necessary and are consistent with his or her nature.

To do that you must learn how to create characters whose emotions are consistent with their actions. Many works are worth studying to see how different authors accomplish this end.

DEATH AT SEA

I recommend two works in particular here, not because either one is necessarily better than any of the others, but because the works themselves were written in such a way as to "isolate" the character dynamic, which makes it easier to study and understand the internal mechanism of character in conflict.

By "isolation" I mean the author takes his or her characters and confines them to what amounts to a vacuum. I already mentioned *2001: A Space Odyssey* by Arthur C. Clarke, in which the three major characters are isolated in space. This design has always been popular in horror and science fiction novels and films (note the merchant ship "Nostromo" in the film *Alien*, or the house in "The Fall of the House of Usher," in which confinement, pushed to the verge of claustrophobia, doubles the tension). The two stories I recommend for you to read are Ernest Hemingway's "The Short Happy Life of Francis Macomber," in which the three characters are isolated by virtue of being on safari in the middle of Africa, and Herman Melville's *Billy Budd*.

Billy Budd creates a triangle of three men. The men are aboard ship at sea, and therefore isolated as the characters in Hemingway's and Clarke's works. The story itself is simple (as great stories often are).

The scene is set in the late eighteenth century, with England at war with France, just after the Great Mutiny at Nore, which was sternly suppressed by the British admiralty.

Into this "letter of the law" Navy comes seaman Billy Budd, a simple-minded, blue-eyed innocent, a "child-man" who is utterly naive when it comes to the ways of the world. He is illiterate, inarticulate, and prone to stutter when pushed.

Enter John Claggart, the ship's master-at-arms, who is as innately evil as Billy is innately good. A clash between the two is inevitable. Claggart falsely accuses Billy of conspiring to overthrow the ship, a charge which no one, not even the Captain, believes. But when Captain Vere confronts Billy with the charge against him and asks Billy to defend himself, Billy is so flabbergasted by the malicious accusation that all he can do is babble.

Claggart, sensing blood, closes in for the kill, but Billy, frustrated by his inability to defend himself with words, instead defends himself with violence, and strikes Claggart a blow that kills him on the spot.

Captain Vere, who doesn't believe Billy is guilty of Claggart's charge of mutiny, and who recognizes Billy's inherent goodness, is now confronted with the most difficult decision of his life. Billy is guilty of striking and killing a superior officer on a warship during wartime. His duty, by the letter of the law, is clear: Billy must hang.

But to hang Billy Budd would be a miscarriage of justice, the extinction of good. Billy Budd's story is indeed a calamity of innocence. As a man, what should Vere do? As the Captain of one of His Majesty's vessels, what must he do? A crisis of conscience.

I put forth the story in half a page. The characters themselves, however, have kept critics and philosophers busy for decades. Billy Budd's character, or John Claggart's, or Captain Vere's can't be reduced to half a page. Melville had a gift for creating characters that can't be pigeon-holed as simple character types. Their complexity makes them unfathomable, mysterious. We can't put our finger on exactly who they are, and why they act the way they do. That's why they intrigue us—because they defy simple analysis. These kinds of characters grow beyond the page: they seem to take on a life of their own. Captain Vere, Claggart, and Billy Budd are absolutely right for the story Melville wants to tell. It would be hard to think of any other character who would fit into this intricate web of good and evil. Compare *Billy Budd* to any of the simple-minded situation comedies on television. Those characters have no soul; they exist only for the quick and easy joke. They can't live beyond the moment, and so they're forgettable. But the dark, brooding characters on Melville's ship make us wonder. . . .

Tolstoy once made a remark about characterization that has always stayed with me and is worth passing along. The comment is one of those pithy observations that rings true not only about fiction, but also about life. To paraphrase Tolstoy, good fiction doesn't come out of the basic conflict of good versus bad. Instead, it comes out of a conflict between *good and good*.

Good versus bad is easy. We know who *should* win; we know whom to root for. The sides are clearly drawn; we know the ground rules, and we're guided by our sense of what's fair, our sense of justice.

Ask yourself what happens, however, when two equally good forces come into conflict with one another, when there is no clear bad guy to hoot, when both sides of the conflict draw out our sympathies. What happens when a couple with a child decide to divorce and end up in a custody battle for their only child *when both husband and wife are victims,* when both love their child, and both are good parents? (*Kramer vs. Kramer*) We know from the start there can be no deserving or undeserving winner, no deserving or undeserving loser. We feel for both parties. Life, we remind ourselves, is like that. We're no longer certain of what's fair.

This is the essence of tragedy.

In *Billy Budd,* Melville explores the tragic complications of the situation aboard the H.M.S. *Bellipotent.* Wait, you say, Billy Budd is good and Claggart is evil; isn't this a story about good versus evil?

The point would be valid if it weren't for the third side of the character triangle, Captain Vere, who is the ultimate focus of the story (but not in the film, which is its flaw). The moral dilemma of the story is the Captain's dilemma: how does one punish the innocent? An innocent who is technically guilty, because Billy *does* kill Claggart.

Neither are the characters of Billy and Claggart drawn as stock caricatures of good and evil. Billy is consecutively described as the Christ, Adam before the Fall, an "upright barbarian," and even a dog. He may be simple-minded, but he's a complex character, evidenced by his fatal flaw, his imperfection of speech, which drives him to murder. Billy may have a pure heart, but he lacks intellect, and is therefore out of balance with the civilized world. He not only lacks evil, he also lacks the ability to discern evil. Billy's dark side is his child-like view of the world as good without the threat of evil: he just doesn't understand the nature of the conflict of good and evil.

Claggart's dark side is much more expansive, but he too is not just a vaudeville villain. In a sense, he's the other side of Billy. Where Billy lacks intellect, Claggart lacks heart. He's as out of balance as Billy, and that's his flaw.

Claggart clashes with Billy. Both men become victims: Billy of Claggart's scheme to destroy him, and Claggart of Billy's primitive defense. Only Captain Vere is left, and he, ultimately, becomes the third victim of the tragedy.

Captain Vere possesses both intellect and heart. He lacks the fatal flaws of the other two men. It is precisely the fact that Captain Vere is balanced that makes his decision regarding Billy so difficult. Again, there can be no winner, only losers. Whatever decision the Captain makes will be a wrong decision, because there is no clear right decision, and yet he must choose.

The Captain doesn't shy from his responsibility. He convenes a drumhead court and by necessity finds Billy guilty and sentences him to hang.

Is this a story about the brutal impersonality of the modern state, that demands the death of the innocent? Or is this a story about society's need to protect itself at all costs in order to ensure order? Either side can be argued effectively.

What's important is Captain Vere's struggle—that of a man's private conscience in conflict with his official responsibility. As the Captain, he must uphold military duty, but as a man, he realizes the sacrifice he must make to the system. At the trial, the Captain argues for the necessity of Billy's conviction, and yet he feels deeply for the innocent sailor, who is a victim of a world he cannot understand.

Billy dies with the Captain's name on his lips. He shouts "God bless Captain Vere," as the hangman fits the noose around his neck. And some time later, as Captain Vere lies dying in battle, he too dies with Billy's name on his lips.

A sign of remorse? Guilt? Not so, says a witness to the Captain's death. Awe, perhaps, or even affection.

The reason I've spent so much time talking about *Billy Budd* is because of the exquisite way Melville plays out the story with his three major characters. The personalities of the characters are woven together as tightly as the design in a Persian carpet.

Nowhere else is character so clearly action, and action so clearly plot. Each is a perfect translation of the other. In addition, Melville's characterizations are not broad strokes of good man, bad man. He creates characters of depth, through detail and specific action. He employs a technique known as Janusian thinking, which is the basis of true, convincing, and effective characters.

Janusian thinking is named after the Roman two-faced god, Janus. We all know what being two-faced means, but here it has a broader application. Being two-faced means that a character has a common, public face, the one we see every day at work and on the streets, and a hidden, private face, which we rarely ever see but which is every bit as much a part of the character as the public face. The two are very often contradictory.

Eugene O'Neill told a story (which he swore was true) that is a wonderful example of a Janusian character. He was having drinks with a man who'd been his roommate in college many years before. After getting a bit oiled, O'Neill's roommate confided a secret that affected the playwright so deeply that he ended up using it as the model of one of the major characters in *The Iceman Cometh*.

"I couldn't take it if my wife ever cheated on me," O'Neill's friend confided. "It would drive me crazy if she did."

We have all read stories and seen films with the theme of jealousy before. Nothing new here. But it's what O'Neill's ex-roommate added that showed the other face, the dark side, the part of the human character that doesn't fit into rational equations: "But there's something inside me," the friend continued, "that wants her to have an affair with another man. I want her to cheat on me."

Doesn't make sense, right? In one breath he says he couldn't stand it if his wife cheated on him, and in the next breath, he confesses that he hopes she does. Two faces, each in complete contradiction with the other. Human personality is that way, and readers recognize the painful condition of humanity by its illogical complications. Billy Budd is this sort of character, and so is Claggart. Both are two-faced; both commit a crime. Both force Captain Vere into making a decision that is two-faced, and ultimately he is forced to commit a crime too. He is not guilty according to martial law, of course, because he has performed his duty. His crime is a moral one, and if he is accountable to anyone, it is to God and himself. Captain Vere puts his country before Billy or himself; in his mind he has no other choice. But at what cost? To condemn Billy is to sacrifice goodness; to free Billy is to condone murder and disorder during dangerous times. Just as O'Neill's roommate loses no matter whether his wife remains faithful or not, so Captain Vere (and all of us) lose; there are no winners. Life's more difficult problems don't always offer solutions. They do, however, demand that we make decisions.

WITHOUT WAX

The following suggestions are guidelines for developing your major characters so that they mesh properly in the patterns of action and plot. This mesh, or weave, if you will, is your goal as an author: a sort of writer's trinity, three-in-one. Character-action-plot. Action is the bridge between the other two. What a character does should, by those actions, construct plot.

To accomplish that, you must do the following:

1. *Develop the character's emotions so they are consistent with his or her character.* From the moment you introduce a character, you establish a pattern of behavior, an important part of which is his or her emotional range. If your character is calculating and cold-blooded, then remain consistent to that emotional range *unless* you can convince the audience (usually by crisis) that this same unfeeling character is capable of tenderness or compassion. The point is to surprise us as readers. Johnny-one-note characters have no chance to surprise us. But as the writer you must also convince us that the unexpected contradiction is possible. No unexplained rabbits out of a hat here. No miracle cures.

2. *Develop your characters so that they become powerful enough to sustain the action.* What kind of character is appropriate for the dramatic phases of your plot pattern? Weakly drawn or clichéd

characters just don't interest us. They are predictable, boring. Yet your characters ought to contain common traits, so that we share a common ground with them and can therefore identify with them, and they should contain *un*common traits so they pop out at us, seem real, convincing.

3. *Develop your major characters so they rise above the simplistic and the generalized.* This point, although closely related to number two, focuses on complexity of character in the way Billy Budd, John Claggart, and Captain Vere are each complex characters. Your major characters should have that certain something, that paradox of behavior that keeps us from understanding them completely. It is part mystery of human behavior, and part paradox. People aren't always predictable and neither should characters be predictable. We are fascinated by what we can't put our finger on; a strong character always somehow manages to elude us, often at the last second, when we think we understand him or her completely. When it comes to people, as it is in life, so it should be in your fiction.

4. *Make your characters sincere.* This suggestion was originally made by Aristotle, and no one's really sure what he meant by "sincere," but I'll give you my version.

The word "sincere" may come from the Latin words *sine*, meaning "without" and *cera*, meaning "wax."

Without wax? It seems there were as many con-men in the Roman marketplace 2,000 years ago as there are now in ours. Shady Roman stoneworkers, lacking the convenience of power tools, would rough-polish marble and then wax the stones to make them look shiny and smooth. The honest dealers, who polished their marble to a mirror finish, would advertise their stone as *sine cera*, "without wax," meaning the real McCoy.

Characters must convince us; they must be "without wax," and the only way you can accomplish that feat is the way the Roman stoneworkers did — with elbow grease. Don't rely on caricatures or stock figures; they are the gimmicks of the con-man and sooner or later will be discovered.

An old stage actor's joke makes the point. An actor, an amateur, was alone on stage delivering Hamlet's famous monologue,

"Alas, poor Yorick . . ." He was awful. His thick Southern drawl, his complete lack of understanding of the character, and his cornball delivery were turning a tragedy into a farce.

The audience started to boo, the actor got even worse, and the booing got louder. Finally the actor, totally exasperated, turned to the audience, held up his hands, and shouted, "Hey, don't blame me, I didn't write this stuff!"

In this case it was the performer, not the character, who was insincere. But your characters perform according to the lines you give them, and if you aren't capable of sincerity, then they won't be either.

The secret of success for characterization lies in their sincerity. If you, as the author, don't believe in your characters, then your characters will lack sincerity. They themselves must believe in what they're doing, no matter how stupid, evil, or pointless it may seem to other characters or to the reader. Sincerity lies in the author's conviction in the character's beliefs. You have to make the investment of belief for all major characters. Otherwise they are nothing more than shadows, obvious tools of the author to make the plot happen.

5. *Make your plot follow the characters; don't let your characters follow the plot.* No matter how brilliant your idea is, if your characters are flat, then your story will be flat. William Faulkner advised a young writer, "If you are going to write, write about human nature." Plot is a means; the exploration of humanity, of the human spirit, is the end. And that can only be done through character.

Plot and characterization are so closely related that at times it's tough to separate the two. You choose the characters because of the plot you've chosen, so in that sense the characters do follow the plot. But once the characters take the stage, they bring their own style and concerns to the page. In effect they become responsible for the plot and take charge of it. You become their slave. If you've created sincere characters, they will lead the way. This often means (but not always) that your plot will change in either small or large ways. They introduce the unexpected.

They lead the way through the twists and turns, surprising you as much as the reader. As the author, you aren't forcing the characters to conform to the plot; rather the characters are forcing you to conform to their plot. And if literary history has any lesson for authors, it's that their characters almost always know best.

CHAPTER 7

PATTERN IN THOUGHT: THEME

DANGER: CONSTRUCTION ZONE

Let's return to the Egyptian architect who first thought of the idea of the true pyramid and equate the process of building the Great Pyramid of Khufu (remember him?) with the equally difficult task of constructing a good story.

First, an *idea*. Except that ideas are like the wind; they have force, they have energy, but they rarely have much shape. The architect knew he wanted to build something on a grand scale, something that had never been done before (or since), something that would last forever. A tomb for his pharaoh. Something first rate, something that would wow the world.

Second, an *audience*. He was building for his pharaoh, and if he couldn't convince him, then he might as well go home. He had to know his audience, he had to know how to surprise and intrigue him, so he developed a *strategy*.

"Listen, Khufu, when the day comes for you to die (may the gods forbid), you want to be *ready*. You want your cousins in heaven to know you've *arrived*. You want them to know you were the greatest king Egypt ever had. Impress the gods. Impress *everyone*."

"How?" asked Khufu.

The architect knew then he had hooked the pharaoh. But he hadn't landed him yet. "With this," he whipped out a sketch of the pyramid and showed it to him.

"Impossible." Khufu shook his head. "It can't be done."

"Yes, it can," tantalized the architect.

"How?"

Now the architect really had the pharaoh's attention. "I'll show you how," he promised, as he laid out the blueprints in front of Khufu.

"How are you going to build this?" Khufu wasn't one to give in easily.

The architect explained each phase of construction. "First we quarry about six million tons of stone . . ."

"What do you mean, *we?*" demanded the king.

"Not you and me," clarified the architect. "We put to work all the people hanging around in the off-season between crops, let them do it."

And so it went. From idea to strategy to sketch (what is it? — the pattern of structure) to blueprints (what's it going to look like? — pattern of plot) to construction plan (how are we going to build it? — the pattern of action) to manpower (who's going to build it? — the pattern of character).

Then came the difficult question: *Why?*

That's what this chapter is about.

The question of *why?* is at the core of every story. Why are you telling this story? What's the point? The question of *why?* separates the physical act of construction from the philosophical reason for doing it. It moves us into a completely different and much more subtle (but just as difficult) realm.

Why? isn't just icing on the cake. Nor is it something you figure out after it's done. The nameless Egyptian architect who told the pharaoh Khufu why the king needed such a grand tomb ("You want your cousins in heaven to know you've *arrived*") wasn't really giving the king the real *why?* of such a massive undertaking. He was only making an argument he thought would sway the pharaoh. The real *why?* is much more profound than a simple appeal to one man's vanity. It has to do with a spectacular convergence of culture and science, combining elegant expressions of religion, philosophy, sociology, mathematics, architecture, and manual artistry into a single object that represents boldly the vision and strength of its builders. So strong is that expression of idea that to this day is still grips our imagination. The pyramid is an impossible feat made possible, and it survives, only slightly battered by history, as a momument to a king and a testament to a people.

The Egyptian architect could have answered truthfully, when he was asked *why?*, that he wanted to build the Great Pyramid because he saw it as the crowning achievement of Egypt, persuasive testimony for future generations that this was a great nation.

And how do you make that testimony? By heaping together six million rocks in the middle of the desert? No, of course not. You make it by the elegance and the precision of its statement.

The builders knew from Rock One what they wanted to say and how they wanted to say it. But the architects already had a thousand years of pyramid building behind them: this was hardly a new invention. It was a refinement of an old idea.

Writing is a tradition thousands of years old also, but any similiarity between pyramid construction and writing ends there. We enter our works much less absolutely and less certainly than the architect enters his. Our ideas are subject to change. They grow; they wither; they change from one state into another, from a caterpillar into . . . what? A Viceroy butterfly? A death's-head moth? An ugly black beetle? Words are not rocks, and neither are ideas.

How then can you control the ideas in your work? How can you give them shape and direction so they don't run all over the place like ants in panic? How do you focus a process as slippery as writing so that the ideas mesh, so they unite like the stones of the pyramid, into an elegant and precise whole?

We're back at *why?* Why am I doing this? One motive: to get rich and become famous. Another motive: to write a work of literature that will keep people marveling for decades. Two entirely different motives, each of which will affect what you write and how you write it. Well, you say, why can't I have both? Fine, that too will affect what you write and how you write it. Any motive will.

Examine your motives. Be honest with yourself. Decide which road you want to travel. Answer the question *why?* Your answer will help you decide how to develop the pattern of thought in your work, which is *theme*. Up to this point we are like the architect who has concentrated only on the technical problems of construction. The time must come—and it should come early in your work—when the aesthetic side of the work must express itself. Writers who ignore the *why?* either end up with a garbled version of the answer or no answer at all.

The word "theme" makes people nervous. Maybe it's because most of us have bad memories about the "themes" we had to write in high school. (Remember your teacher handing out assignments? "Write a five-hundred-word theme about your most embarrassing moment.") The theme I'm talking about isn't the theme the teacher was talking about.

We should begin with a kind of working definition in order to clear up the air about what theme is and how it works. Theme, for our purposes here anyway, is the *central concern* around which a story is structured. Sometimes you hear that theme is the "message" of the story, the point, the central idea, or the statement of the story, but that's too confining and doesn't always work.

Theme is your inertial guidance system. It directs your decisions about which path to take, which choice is right for the story and which choice isn't. As we write, we only start to understand the actual meaning of the work, but with theme, we actually structure the work on a *concept* that guides us from the start.

Theme shouldn't be some fuzzy, in-the-back-of-your-mind idea, but a viable, working pattern, like the others in this book. As with plots, there are several types of patterns into which all works fall, but, unlike plot patterns, there aren't nearly as many. Choosing the theme that best suits the story you want to tell will help you express your idea clearly.

The idea of theme comes from what we may call priority of technique. Almost every work contains the major elements of storytelling: plot, character, style, idea, and mood, or emotional effect. These five elements do not always have the same priority in the work. Sometimes plot is more important than character, and sometimes character is more important than plot. Any one of the five elements of plot, character, mood, style, or idea can dominate the others. The element that does dominate the work is said to be the work's *theme*.

Let's examine each major pattern of theme more closely.

1. Plot As Theme: Goldfinger Meets Miss Marple

We are action junkies. We like to have things happen, and we like for them to happen fast and furiously. We like to escape the humdrum pattern of everyday life. So a lot of us read books to escape the drabness of our workaday world. The theme of escapist literature is just that: escape. We can, on the turning of a page, go on the hunt, join the chase, stalk the prey. These works aren't serious works of literature, and they aren't meant to be.

In these works everything, including character, becomes secondary to action and plot, all of which moves to the final outcome, *the grand finale*.

The pattern is typical of everything from the James "007" Bond novels to the Conan series, from pure action-adventure films such as *Raiders of the Lost Ark* and *Indiana Jones and the Last Crusade* to *Die Hard*. Even stylist Agatha Christie novels fall into this pattern of theme.

Because such little premium is placed upon people or ideas, we categorize these works as popular literature. The author makes no serious attempt at social comment, no real delving into the human condition. Outside the context of the story, the people and events have little meaning in our own lives. However much we enjoy these works and look forward to the next one, their effect is momentary. We read, we enjoy, we forget, and read another one.

Obviously these books comprise a big chunk of the commercial market. Success for some is measured on the bestseller list and at the box office. These books and films make money — a lot of money. Ripping yarns have always held us hypnotized from the days of fireside storytellers to the computerized book-of-the-month clubs. They have an important place in the spectrum of literature, but success depends on understanding the basic function of the work: to allow the reader to escape into a world that he ordinarily would never otherwise know.

2. Effect As Theme: *Friday the 13th, Part XXII*

Another very large section of the commercial market belongs to this category. The main focus of the pattern changes from events to emotional effect. Certain types of books and films strive primarily for a certain emotional effect that the reader or viewer expects to experience in the work. That effect may be terror (as in the case of any Stephen King or John Carpenter work), suspense (as in the case of the works of Robert Ludlum, Robin Cook, or Alfred Hitchcock), love and romance (as in the case of any Harlequin or Silhouette novel) or comedy.

Comedy has never done as well in literature as it has in film. We expect humorists from Charlie Chaplin to Mel Brooks to be funny and so we look forward to their works as such. If they try to step out of character we tend to be very intolerant. Charlie Chaplin once made a movie in which he played a serial killer (*Monsieur Verdoux*), and audiences couldn't deal with their sweet Charlie playing a serious dramatic role as a man who marries women for their money and then murders them. The film, actually one of Chaplin's better ones, was a box-office flop, and to this day is still obscure.

Look at the problem Woody Allen had converting from his early silly films (*Sleeper, Bananas, Everything You Wanted to Know About Sex but Were Afraid to Ask*) to his later serious films (*Manhattan, Interiors, Hannah and Her Sisters*). We resisted the change because we wanted Chaplin and Allen and Stephen King to write what we expect of them. We want them to make us laugh or to scare us the same way they did in the past.

If you choose effect as your theme, then concentrate on that effect in your work. Study your successful rivals and see how they did it. It is also possible to combine more than one effect in a work with success. No doubt by now you've heard the word "dramedy" — Hollywood's buzzword for stories that are half drama and half comedy, in films such as *Silver Streak* and *Midnight Run*.

Combining effects has its dangers. One shouldn't work at the expense of the other. Note the way horror and comedy were mixed in *An American Werewolf in London*. It shocks *and* it makes us laugh, all in the right places. It's a precarious balance, because the audience could end up laughing where it was supposed to be frightened, and that's a death blow to any work. John Irving combines drama and comedy effectively in *The World According to Garp*. As in Plot As Theme, make sure you understand the expectations of your audience before you write your story.

3. Style As Theme: Poetry in Motion

With this category we depart sharply from the mainstream commercial market and focus on a small minority of books and films in which the author's style becomes the focus of the work. The work may still include all the basic elements of good storytelling, but plot, character, and action take a back seat to this expression of style.

Of course every novel and film has its own style, but in this case the style of the piece has such a profound effect that everything else is seen through it. It acts as a colored lens through which everything is shot.

The bulk of American readers and moviegoers have limited patience when it comes to tolerating such an elevated artistic technique. John Hawkes, considered by many to be one of the best living authors in the United States today, has been writing for forty years and is virtually unknown in this country except in universities and by other writers. In France, however, where style is appreciated by a larger segment of the general public, Hawkes is very popular. Books like *The Lime Twig* and *Second Skin* are the perfection of individualized style over stock-in-trade elements of plot and character.

The pattern holds the same for film. Works such as *Days of Heaven*, *Angel Heart*, and *Three Women* or the works of Federico Fellini or Ingmar Bergman bear the unmistakable stamp of author (and director, of course).

4. Character As Theme: The Making of Mr. and Mrs. Right

Literature is full of books about people. When a work concentrates on a person (or persons) so that he or she (or they) become the center of plot and action, then the theme of the work is character. *David Copperfield, Madame Bovary, Anna Karenina, Raging Bull* and *The Great Santini* are just a few examples of many. Just look in your library for books with people's names in the titles.

We are fascinated by other people. Nonfiction biographies have always sold well, and so do fiction books and films about unique people who capture our imagination. These works delve in the core of character, into an examination of the human spirit. The character is at once the plot and the action. Remember the story in Chapter 4 about the boy who accidentally kills his brother in a hunting accident? I gave two versions based on different plot patterns. In the first version, the story concentrated on Jonathan, the younger brother. The theme of that story would be character as we explore the effects of action (the accident) on Jonathan's character.

In the second version, the plot pattern shifted from "Remorse" to "Kinsman Kills Unrecognized Kinsman," but does the theme change? No. The theme remains the same, except that instead of focusing on Jonathan alone, we concentrate upon the effect of the tragedy on the family as a whole.

Writing about people (as the theme) is richly rewarding. As opposed to Plot As Theme and Effect As Theme, which don't ordinarily lend themselves to serious literary treatment (but do offer larger audiences), this theme pattern manages to combine both if you wish.

The perfect example in American literature, said to be *The Great American Novel* (the one we always hoped to write, right?) is *The Adventures of Huckleberry Finn*. Part of the reason for its success is that Twain, the consummate storyteller, combined penetrating characterization with serious literary treatment.

We are often told that if a book is literary then it won't sell, and if it does sell, then it's not literary.

If there is any truth to that statement (and there is some), the problem lies more with the author's belief that it's true than with any actual truth of the matter. It's certainly more true of Plot as Theme, but less true of Character As Theme. A book worth reading that was a huge international best seller, which has the character of several generations of a family as its theme, is Gabriel Garcia Marquez' *One Hundred Years of Solitude*. Garcia Marquez has since gone on to win the Nobel Prize for literature; proof that you *can* write and sell well.

The theme patterns we've discussed so far are more limiting than Character As Theme, which opens up all kinds of possibilities in the full range of writing.

5. *Idea As Theme: It's the Thought that Counts*

Of the other four theme patterns, none succeeds as well as this pattern in creating events and characters of significance that reach far beyond the words printed on the page. These are the works that affect us profoundly, make us think, perhaps even change our lives. Over history, works from this category have been the ones to change the world: start and stop wars, cause revolution and incite riots, expose cruelty, abuse, and stupidity in government, in the marketplace, and in the privacy of our homes. They are found on the shelves of every library and bookstore, including the children's sections. We flourish on ideas, new and old. They make us reach beyond our grasp.

A book like *Robinson Crusoe*, for example, is a book of ideas. Because of the title you might think that the character of the shipwrecked sailor was the theme of the novel, but *Robinson Crusoe* is more about ideas than it is about a person who gets stranded on an island. The same is true of *Don Quixote*.

It is worth pointing out here that film adaptations of novels (like *Robinson Crusoe* and *Don Quixote*) routinely alter the theme of the original work for the screen. While the plot pattern remains the same, and the characters stay the same (more or less), the theme pattern often shifts from the more difficult (and less cinematic) Idea As Theme to the easier (and more exciting) Plot As Theme. This is the reason why so many people who have read the book are disappointed with the movie version: the ideas have been wrung out of the original. (There are some notable exceptions. For example, *Shane* and *The Graduate* are both better than the original work in print.)

Ideas can take many different forms as they shape the thematic content of your work. The list that follows includes only the major themes, all of which you will recognize. These ideas can't always be expressed in a single word or a sentence. They are often complicated concepts that affect characters and plot on a continuing and changing basis throughout your work.

In the discussion about *Billy Budd* for instance, whose theme falls under this category, I proposed two common interpretations of the work, *and they were at complete odds with each other*. Some readers believe the story is about the cruelty of the system (the British navy, society in general) that will slaughter innocence (represented by the character of Billy) in order to protect itself. It's a cynical view, but one that can be argued powerfully.

On the other hand, someone not quite as cynical could come back with an argument just as powerful—that in order for a system to survive (we're back to talking about society) it must make rules to protect itself, and in the long run it is best for all even if, from time to time, a person gets caught in the cracks and is sacrificed by the system to make it work. This is the cost of civilization, and perhaps this is closest to what Captain Vere himself believed.

Is the cost too expensive? Some will say yes and others will say no. Which is the correct interpretation for the story, the first or the second version? Or maybe there's a third way or even a fourth way of looking at the story. What did Melville think? Does it really matter?

No, it doesn't. *Billy Budd* contains ideas, and the whole point of ideas is to think about them, discuss them, and reach our own conclusions. As an author you can't force your audience to think a certain way, but you can make your audience think *about* your ideas.

Here are the major categories into which most Ideas As Theme fall:

a. The Moral Statement: Now hear this!

Any work that spends the major part of its energy to persuade us to accept a certain moral principle would fall under the category of Moral Statement as theme.

The danger of this category is that too many writers love to get on a soapbox and preach. They'll do anything to wax philosophical and talk about the meaning of good and evil in the universe. They use the fiction as an excuse to tell the world what they think. Their characters never come to life, and their plots are flat and unconvincing.

These writers ought not to be writing fiction. If they feel so strongly about their ideas and want to put them to paper, they should write nonfiction, which is much more suited to sermonizing.

Of course there is nothing wrong with sermonizing in either fiction or nonfiction. The problem is that in the case of fiction, at least, the author methodically promotes a point of view at the cost of storytelling; this is the definition of propaganda.

But if the plot is gripping and the characters believable and sincere, and if you're interested in telling a story (as opposed to using fiction simply as a format for your ideas), then the "moral" of the story should hit home. Two successful examples from recent film are *Fatal Attraction* (married men shouldn't mess around with strange women) and *Wall Street* (greed is bad). Both stories work because the writers were more interested in their characters than in the moral message itself. The ideas and the morals were the *result* of the story. In propaganda, the story and the character are the result of the idea. They become a means rather than what they should be: an end in themselves.

b. Human Dignity: "I y'am what I y'am."

Suppose you were a bit odd. Not dangerous, not crazy, at least not in the clinical sense, just off-beat. You don't fit comfortably into the role of a John or Jane Doe. And suppose you suddenly found yourself locked in a mental ward so your behavior could be "observed." Around you are some of the truly sick, mentally unbalanced people who cannot cope with the real world. And suppose still that the nurse in charge of your ward is intent on making you conform—perhaps the word should be submit rather than conform—to her tyrannical system of care?

An absolute nightmare. Ken Kesey wrote the book (later

made into the film) *One Flew Over the Cuckoo's Nest,* a powerful and harrowing story of one man's fight for dignity and the right to be who he was in the face of a system that set out to destroy him.

The struggle for human dignity is one of humankind's basic conflicts, one that we think and write about a lot. We have a base, animal side to us: brutal, selfish, and powerful. We also have a higher spiritual side: caring, giving, and intelligent. Works in this category explore both sides, and the costs of both. Usually the central characters, like McMurphy in *One Flew Over the Cuckoo's Nest,* are put at a disadvantage and have to struggle for their right to be who they want to be.

The struggle may be external, as in McMurphy's fight against dehumanization in the institution, which is usually a metaphor for society as a whole. The same story is true in Lina Wertmuller's haunting film, *Seven Beauties,* about a man who is a petty criminal sent to a concentration camp during World War II. What must he do to survive? And what will the cost be?

Always there is a cost to be paid. Often a heavy cost. And we are left to wonder if such a heavy cost is worth the struggle.

The struggle may be internal also, such as a character who recognizes his or her own weaknesses as a human being and has to confront those demons that live inside. Anyone who's ever seen Marlon Brando play the down-and-out boxer Terry Malloy in *On the Waterfront* will never forget his speech, "I coulda had class . . . I coulda been a contender . . . I coulda been *somebody!*"

Sylvester Stallone borrowed Rocky Balboa (*Rocky I-IV*) from Terry Malloy as Rocky struggles to be "somebody," to find dignity, but the movies are shallow on ideas and long on schlock.

c. Social Comment: They Don't Make Them Like They Used To

We live in a huge kettle of people. Our society, however much we're attached to it, has its problems, and writers like to address these problems in the hopes we will pay attention to them and perhaps even do something to make this a better world. American literature has many great examples, among them novels like *The Grapes of Wrath*, *Elmer Gantry*, and *The Octopus*.

As with the Moral Statement, writers get tempted by the urge to preach when it comes to talking about the ills of society. The golden rule of writing, *show, don't tell*, is never more true than here.

There is a famous story about a French Impressionist painter and a famous French Symbolist poet that underscores the basic problem writers have when the idea becomes more important than the story. The Painter and the Poet were in a cafe arguing:

"You writers have it easy," scoffed the Painter. "All you need is a few good ideas and a pen." He waved his hand in a wide arc as if to dismiss the Poet. "Now, *painting* is hard. Every brush-stroke is one-of-a-kind, not like words—they're always the same."

"If it's so easy, why don't you write some poems?" challenged the Poet.

"All right, I will." The Painter accepted the challenge, downed his absinthe, and steamed off to his studio to write his great poems.

Several weeks went by before the Poet bumped into the Painter at their favorite watering hole. From the Painter's sheepish grin, the Poet guessed things weren't going so well for his friend.

"Written any good poems lately?" the Poet taunted.

"I don't understand it," confessed the Painter, still puzzled by his aborted attempt to write poetry. "I had good ideas. They just wouldn't turn out right on paper."

"That's because you don't start with ideas," the Poet smiled knowingly. "You begin with words."

The Poet was saying that strong stories generate their own ideas, not the other way around. The story and the characters always come first. Abstract intellectual concepts for ideas will put a story back on the poisoned path of propaganda.

So if you want to criticize our society, if you want to wave a red flag or suggest change, then find the story to tell it. The author of *The China Syndrome* wanted to warn us about the dangers of a nuclear meltdown, and at the time we weren't too interested in the message, at least not until real life stepped in — as it does at the oddest times — and we were reading headlines in the newspaper about Three Mile Island. Suddenly the message was urgent and the warning of *The China Syndrome* was very real.

And yet the storyline of *The China Syndrome* holds its own. The author wasn't crusading. The plot was intriguing, the characters were reasonably interesting, and the tension and suspense kept our interest. The author resisted the impulse to use one of the characters as his own mouthpiece; he let the characters speak for themselves out of their own roles in the story. True, the character played by Jane Fonda — and to an extent the character played by Jack Lemmon — makes speeches about the dangers of nuclear energy, but those speeches come from the character's moral and social conscience rather than directly from the author's.

This lesson is the key to writing successfully if you feel the urge or the need to make social comment in fiction. Steinbeck makes us care about the Joad family in *The Grapes of Wrath*, and the Joads, through their anguish, teach us about America during the Depression, about the poor and the displaced, the wandering homeless in search of the American dream.

Too much propaganda has been written in the guise of fiction. And readers don't like propaganda because the story and the characters lack sincerity. Argue from your characters' convictions, not your own. Don't let the message get ahead of the medium.

d. Human Nature As Theme: Three Men in a Tub

What is Man? A question as much for writers as it is for philosophers; a forum for fiction as much as it is for the treatise, the monograph, or the essay. As writers, part of our job is to explore the nature of humanity, either through individuals (Characters As Theme) or through a broader view of people and humanity in general.

The difference between Character As Theme and Idea As Theme (Human Nature) is that in the former category, the character in the work is particularized. One-of-a-kind. We don't see anyone we really recognize, but we are intrigued by the character's uniqueness.

In this category of theme, however, the main character or characters of the story represent universal human types. We do recognize the people, although we may not recognize their circumstances.

These characters, and their crises, reach beyond the page because they represent our view of civilization, of humankind in general. William Golding's brilliant and gripping novel, *Lord of the Flies*, takes a group of very proper British schoolboys and strands them on an uninhabited island without adults. Before long the children, forced to create their own society, drop any pretense of a polite, genteel society and revert to a savage, brutal system in their struggle for power and survival.

Robinson Crusoe, a story about a shipwrecked sailor who must confront the difficulties of a solitary and primitive existence, also explores what it means to be a human, and what it means to be civilized. Note that in both works, the characters are again isolated, cut off from others without any real hope of help.

The same is true for the cast of characters in James Dickey's *Deliverance*. Isolated in the Appalachian backwoods, several men from middle-class suburbia suddenly find themselves confronted by a harsh, cruel environment that forces them to confront truths about themselves (and perhaps about us all).

e. Human Relations As Theme: Looking for Love in All the Wrong Places

This theme pattern is kin to the last one. In that pattern, the author is concerned with understanding who we are as people, whereas in this pattern the focus shifts to examining the difficulties people have when it comes to getting along with one another, *especially* when it comes to complex, intimate relationships that occur in love, in marriage, and in the family.

These stories hit close to home. We all know to some degree the difficulties of developing, keeping, or dissolving relationships. We've read a ton of books and seen as many movies about starting up or starting over, of marriages under fire, of working through all the domestic crises that trouble us.

Sometimes the stories are painful, as in *Ordinary People*, as a family tries to cope with the death of a son and finds that it has to redefine itself. Larry McMurtry's *Terms of Endearment* also explores the strained relationship between mother and daughter and how the daughter's terminal illness forces them to deal with the problems they'd been avoiding.

The stories don't have to be tragic in order to contain the truth. The basic premise behind the play *The Odd Couple* examines the relationship between two men, one compulsively neat, the other compulsively sloppy.

As with Human Nature As Theme, we are brought close to the ideas because of their universality. We all know Oscar Madisons, just as we know Felix Ungars. These stories talk about us as a class of people, as a society, and as a civilization. If you should decide to write a work which has as its theme a study of the pains and/or the rewards of relationships, then you should concentrate on the characters themselves rather than the relationship itself. The relationship comes from character; don't force characters into relationships.

Avoid clichés of character and action, like the story of the brilliant but alcoholic brain surgeon who falls in love with a woman who saves him from his own self-destructiveness, or the story of the mad scientist and his forbidden experiments that result in the creation of a monster. And please, no more vampire stories, unless you can do what Anne Rice does in her *Vampire Chronicles* by throwing out all the tired clichés about vampires and creating characters and situations that are totally new.

Make the people interesting but don't make them bizarre, for that will make our identification with them difficult or even impossible. These should be people we believe we could be ourselves if we found ourselves in a similar position. This theme was the foundation for *The Big Chill*, exploring a web of relationships between college classmates who reunite several years after graduation. Somewhere in those characters we no doubt recognize ourself and our friends; we recognize their problems; we recognize their joy and their grief. In the end, it is just as much a story about us as it is about the fictional characters.

The appeal of universality is that the story works within the realm of possibilities for all of us. If your characters are too much out of the mainstream of people as we know them, then they are apart from us, different, at most entertaining oddities. For this theme to work as an idea, you must reach out and speak to us, your audience, and make us feel the pain and the joy of living with other people.

f. Innocence to Experience: The Way of the World

How often have you heard someone older complain that youth was wasted on the young? We look back to our childhood and remember the awkwardness, the confusion, and best of all, the magic moments of discovery, those "firsts" — our first love, our first sexual experience, our first apartment — as we traveled the rocky road to maturity.

Writers like to explore that road and its various stops along the way. Not simply the events, but the effect of the events on people. These stories are often called "Coming of Age" stories or "Loss of Innocence" stories. *The Summer of '42* and *American Graffiti* are well-known examples.

During the last five years, Hollywood, aware of the size of the youth market, has made an effort to capture it with films about growing up. As evidence, films starring the "Brat Pack": *The Breakfast Club*, *St. Elmo's Fire*, *Pretty in Pink*, and *About Last Night*. This theme pattern is much more common in film than in literature, perhaps because there is no real book market for those same people. The Young Adult (sometimes called "YA") market does address these questions of maturity but in the same shallow, formulaic way that romance novels explore love. This kind of reading is meant to be light, entertaining, and escapist. If the questions are demanding and tough, and if they relate too closely to the discomfort of daily living, then they break the illusion of a world in which our problems always find perfect solutions.

Theme is an element in the heirarchy of technique that develops during the course of the work. We may think we know what our work is really about, but the experience of writing usually changes all our preconceived notions. Picasso pointed to the process of discovery and said that what you actually accomplished during the act of creating was what was important, not what you intended to do. Rarely are the two the same.

As you write, the horizons of your work will constantly open up. You will see new things, think new thoughts, find new directions. The road through the dark forest of confusion is never clear, and we make our choices about which road to take at every juncture, never sure where that road is going to take us. But if you decide on a pattern of theme, you decide on a kind of road-map that you want to follow and it will guide you. Your decisions won't be nearly as blind, and like Dante, who has to negotiate the road through Hell in the *Inferno*, you too will have a guide, your Vergil, to help you through the endless maze.

CHAPTER 8

PATTERN IN PLACE

CROSSROADS OF CIRCUMSTANCE

Time for a quiz. I name an author, you name the place. For example, if I say "Dickens," you should answer "London." Not because Dickens was born or lived in London, but because so many of his works take place there.

Or I name a place, and you name the author associated with the place. So, to give another example, if I say "The Catskill Mountains," you should answer "Washington Irving." (Who can forget Rip Van Winkle or Ichabod Crane?)

First question: Yoknapatawpha County, Mississippi.

If you've ever read this author, you'll know in an instant it's William Faulkner. No doubt about it. Yoknapatawpha County is William Faulkner.

Second question: James Joyce.

The answer sure isn't Miami Beach. James Joyce and Dublin, Ireland, are synonymous.

Third question: Albany, New York.

This one's tougher. But if you've read *Ironweed*, or *Legs* or *Quinn's Book*, you'll know I'm talking about William Kennedy.

Last one: Henry David Thoreau.

Walden Pond, of course.

In each case the author has made the place, the setting of the work so unique that it becomes a major element of the work itself. In Faulkner's imaginary Yoknapatawpha County, he created a complex social structure in which he explored the burden of the Southern past, the failure of the crumbling Southern aristocracy to enter the twentieth century, and the tensions between black man and white man. Could he have done this if he'd set his work in the Napa Valley of California or in Crazy Mountains of Montana? No way.

And what if, instead of retiring to Walden Pond outside of Concord, Thoreau instead decided to study the Port Authority Terminal in New York City? Do you think anybody would be reading his work today? I doubt it.

Each of the authors I mentioned above made something of a place so that it became part of the plot, part of the characters, and part of the theme of the work. They did what Joseph Conrad did to Africa in *Heart of Darkness*, what F. Scott Fitzgerald did to the Paris of the Twenties, what Frank Herbert did for the planet Dune. You can't take *Heart of Darkness* and just exchange Africa for Yugoslavia without making mincemeat of the work. Nor can you trade the Atlantic Ocean for Lake Erie any more than you can change the great white whale for a giant, man-eating perch without turning *Moby Dick* into a farce.

In these works, place is every bit as important as plot or character. It is a strand in the rope of fiction, no more nor any less important than any other strand.

Eudora Welty, one of the *grande dames* of American literature, wrote in her book *Place in Fiction,* "It is by the nature of itself that fiction is all bound up in the local. The internal reason for that is surely that feelings are bound up in places."

Larry McMurtry's *The Last Picture Show* takes place in a desolate, dusty town in West Texas. You can feel the land in the people, in what they think, say, and do. They *are* the land, and, conversely, the land is them. Part of the theme of the novel is place, and place is bound up with the emotions of the characters.

Eudora Welty adds, "Location is the crossroads of circumstance, the proving ground of 'What happened? Who's here? Who's coming?' "

Today many writers underestimate the potential value of setting, and the role it plays in developing the imagination. John Gardner criticized young writers of today for being so influenced by the sameness of life and place as it is portrayed on television. "Many student writers seem unable to tell their most important stories — the death of a father, the first disillusionment of love — except in the molds and formulas of TV," which, he goes on to point out, are totally false.

The towns are bland, the cities are nameless and feel the same even if they have names. A suburb is a suburb is a suburb. Where is Flannery O'Connor's rural Georgia? Saul Bellow's Upper West Side of New York? Places tend to be more like movie set backdrops. Need a beach? Coming up, one generic beach. A lot of sand, a couple of umbrellas, a shovel and a pail, and bingo, you got a beach. Need an apartment? No problem, one apartment coming up: a table, chairs, a TV and a sofa, and bang, you got your basic apartment kit. These locations are like the flats they roll out of storage for sit-coms. Who cares if Ozzie and Harriet's house looks exactly like the Cleavers' house or the Keatons' house? It's mashed potatoes — bland, insipid, and lifeless.

Going Home Again

Within each of us lies a landscape we know intimately. It's a landscape that, as Eudora Welty pointed out, we are tied to emotionally. It is part of us, the same way the Mississippi River was part of Mark Twain. For some of us it's an urban landscape. We know a city, a certain neighborhood in that city. We know who lived where and what happened there. We know the smells of kettles simmering in kitchens with open windows, the smells from the local brewery, and from the pool rooms and corner taverns that always had their front door open, even in winter. We know the sounds too. The sounds of a ballpark from the inside and from the outside. We know the sound of sirens on late night streets. We know the yards, the alleys and breezeways, the courtyards, places above and below ground that only a person who grew up and lived in a city would know. That place is as much a part of us as our skin or our memory. We think it, we feel it, we hate it, and yet we yearn for it.

Chances are you know this place in one form or another. If not the city, then it's the pine barrens of New Jersey or Virginia or Maine, or it's the ohi'a forests of Hawaii. It may be the Delta, the mesas and arroyos, the bayous, or flat-top prairie. This place is part of you; it reaches inside you and speaks to you of history and family and being. You understand the correspondences between the exteriors of place and the interiors of the people who live in that place.

You may have traveled and seen wonderful places and exotic things, but even though you've diligently taken notes about the birds and the flowers and the trees and anything else that caught your fancy, you may not have penetrated the core of the place. These are simply descriptions — they are things — and although things are part of place, they may not be the spirit or the "soul" of the place. Only natives would know the inner world of a place, which details are true and which aren't. Part of your responsibility as a writer is to be sincere, to be convincing — not only about your characters, but about all the aspects of telling a story. You can tell when an author "knows" the setting in which his story is set; you can tell if he's being sincere or is faking it. John Cheever is comfortable with "Shady Hill" and as he reaches inside place, he shows us the heart of American suburbia. James Baldwin knows New York City, but it's an entirely different city from the New York of Bernard Malamud or Edith Wharton or Henry James. Each saw a different face of New York, from Harlem down to Washington Square. And so the stories and the characters in their stories reflect the face of the city they know.

Well, you might argue, Ray Bradbury never went to Mars when he wrote the *Martian Chronicles*, nor Frank Herbert to *Dune*. Stephen Crane had never been on a Civil War battlefield, yet he wrote *The Red Badge of Courage*. The most famous case of all was Sax Rohmer, who was a recluse and never left his West Side apartment in New York City, and yet he wrote the entire series of Fu Manchu novels. How did these authors "know" these places so well if they'd never been to them?

Place is as much an expression of the imagination as it is an observation of actual geography. Your ability to write well about place, to establish a pattern of things and events, depends upon your ability to construct the proper details that give the reader a psychological impression of the meaning of that place, and to convince the reader with those details that the place does indeed exist. Don't throw in a maple tree unless there's a reason for throwing one in. If it's fall, and the sugar maples are a brilliant red, the color of blood, and the relationship between your main characters is about to turn bloody, then you have created an echo, a psychological impression that will foreshadow what's to come. This is an example of how the details of the physical world — place — have to work together with the patterns of character and plot. By doing this you strengthen the work.

Imagine, then, the place where you want your story to be. Make a mental geography. You may even want to draw a map. Where do people live in relation to each other? What are the geographical features that are important to the story, such as a certain mountain, as in Hemingway's *The Snows of Kilimanjaro*, or a river, as the Mississippi in Twain's works. How do those features relate to the actual plot? This is the kind of fertile ground from which symbols sprout. The object or the event mean *more* than what they appear to mean at the surface.

An example. Let's say you were writing a story about a married couple during the last days of their disintegrating relationship. The emotional atmosphere between them is chilled. More than chilled, their hearts are frozen after years of mutual abuse. You have picked a plot and your characters, now you must pick a place for them to happen. The idea of using winter as an emotional parallel is obvious. The freezing wind outside their house parallels the freezing emotional wind inside the house. But suppose you tried to find a way in which to represent the story itself in a single image, an image of place, which foreshadows what is to come. What detail would you choose? Many such details are possible, and I give you only one in order to demonstrate that your story can be told in the straightforward ways of character-in-action, but it can also be told symbolically by your descriptions of place. Let's use the analogy of winter, but find a unique, dramatic, and highly visual representation of it rather than relying on abstraction. Suppose, in the beginning of the story as you describe the town in which this couple lives, you talk about the depth of the cold: "The freeze was so hard that winter that it reached into the heart of the tamarack trees, and late at night we could hear the trees exploding one by one on the edge of the heath." An image like the exploding trees could become a metaphor for the emotional relationship between the characters, which have yet to be introduced, and yet the writer has created an emotional climate that sets the stage for them.

Barry Lopez, author of *Arctic Dreams*, a book about landscape and the imagination, wrote about the interior and exterior landscapes of place. Of the exterior landscape, he writes "One learns a landscape finally not by knowing the name or identity of everything in it, but by perceiving the relationships in it. . . ." There is a sense of cultural and social ecology: knowing the relationships between things and people and place. To be convincing as a writer when it comes to place, you can't just hand over a catalog of details and expect the reader to believe, to feel, to sense in full depth the colors, the smells, the sheer physicality of it. You have to go deeper, beneath the surface of ordinary details, and find what truths lie beneath it. Don't write "It was a big, loud, dirty city." The adjectives, heaped on like thick sauce, are meaningless. All cities are big, loud, and dirty. What is it that's distinct about the place you're writing about that captures the eye and the mind of the reader, that somehow reflects either directly or indirectly (that is, symbolically) what is happening in your story? Catalogs of descriptions only add words. Your job is to delve, to reveal the invisible world.

The interior landscape, Lopez continues, is a "projection within a person of a part of the exterior landscape." Here is the correlation between the two landscapes, the one that exists outside of the people available to the camera, and the one that exists inside the people, invisible to the eye or the ear except in actions and words. "These thoughts are arranged, further, according to the thread of one's moral, intellectual, and spiritual development. The interior landscape responds to the character and subtlety of the exterior one; the shape of the individual mind is affected by land as it is by genes."

Three Beaches

Almost everyone has heard of the Scottish novelist Sir Walter Scott, the author of the romance *Ivanhoe* (or at least has seen the film version starring Robert Wagner). We remember the knight Ivanhoe and his love for Rowena, his father's ward. And we remember Rebecca the Jewess, and Robin Hood as Locksley, and Richard the Lionhearted in the guise of the Black Knight. And a few have read *The Bride of Lammermore* or *Waverly* (which probably has the greatest number of sequels of any work in literary history: thirty-one). But most of us who read Scott got tired of reading him pretty quickly. His plots were too coincidental, the romances became too sweet, and worst of all, we tired of his style. In defense of Scott, he was very popular in his day, and his fans included people like Tolstoy and Balzac, but for today's readers he doesn't make the cut for the twentieth century. His endless descriptions of places and things are enough to tax the patience of anyone who isn't seriously interested in tons of historical detail. When Scott went to the beach on the rugged coast of Scotland, he would describe for you every nook and cranny, every rock, and every bird sitting on every perch. He would give you a complete history of place, cast in the rosy glow of romance, with every sweeping, grandiose gesture in the book. His attention to detail was *painstaking*. You could not leave any place Scott took you to without knowing every square inch of it, whether or not it had anything to do with the story. When the time came for you to move on, you felt as if you'd spent half your life there.

A hundred years ago, before the miracle (or curse) of radio or television, readers didn't mind these massive descriptions of place. For some, who rarely ever got far from the place they were born, it took the place of travel, and they liked reading about all the flora and fauna of other places. What else was there to do on those long, wintry nights? Today, however, we are much more savvy about the world and much less tolerant about travelogs that don't have anything to do with the story. We want our authors to get to the point. We are impatient readers: a lot of us can't stand Sir Walter Scott because we keep muttering under our breath, *Get on with it, man.*

Not far from Scotland, across a short stretch of rough water, lies Ireland. And at the heart of Ireland is Dublin, home of James Joyce. When Joyce writes about the beach, as he does in *Ulysses*, he immediately gets to the heart of the matter. We still see, feel, hear, and smell the place: it appears in our mind's eye, and yet he doesn't make us suffer through ten pages of details. He does it, in fact, in a few well-chosen lines:

> Unwholesome sandflats waited to suck his treading soles, breathing upward sewage breath. . . . A porterbottle stood up, stogged to its waist in the cakey sand dough; at the land a maze of dark cunning nets; farther away chalk-scrawled backdoors and on the higher beach a drying line with two crucified shirts.

Note the vividness and the exactness of Joyce's descriptions. It's not your typical description of Malibu or Waikiki, and it's anything but a backdrop. The details convey tension and pain. The beach is like quicksand as it tries to suck the character in just as it has the wine bottle, "stogged to its waist." Other details speak of danger and death, such as the "dark cunning nets" and the two crucified shirts. What do these things imply? They are sinister and create a dark, foreboding mood, one that's consistent with the main character of the novel.

The exterior landscape — the filthy, "unwholesome" beach, and the interior landscape — the emotional and intellectual content of the character, are linked symbolically through significant detail. These details, the ones that bridge the two landscapes and make the connections between persons, place, and things, obviously go beyond window dressing. They are part of a pattern themselves.

But not a separate pattern. They are part of a pattern that's shaped by the other patterns of character, plot, and action, and in turn, a pattern that itself shapes these things. This is the ecosystem I was talking about earlier. In any ecosystem, each individual and process depends upon every other individual and process in the same system in order to survive. One definition of a work of art confirms this holistic approach to writing. A work of art, the definition goes, is something that will be destroyed if you add anything to it or subtract anything from it.

That is also the definition of balance. Of precarious balance. All the elements work together and create a delicate harmony.

As writers we're always struggling to find that balance, that moment when everything clicks into place, when all the smaller patterns converge to create a single, larger pattern that is the ecosystem of the work.

We usually think of an ecosystem in terms of biology, in terms of living things in relation to the processes within their environment. But it is a small jump to think of an ecosystem in terms of the living things in a story (the characters) in relation to the processes (plot and action) within their environment (the setting). One cannot function adequately without the support of all the others, and the failure of one damages or even destroys the others.

Finally, the last of the three beaches. Return to the Great Pyramid of Khufu and think about the role of setting and its importance to its ecosystem. As one of the ancient Seven Wonders of the World, it would qualify as a work of art under the definition of perfect balance. Time has taken a toll on the limestone face of the pyramid over the centuries, but we can see that once upon a time, at the beginning of recorded history, every stone was in place, and the pyramid was perfectly finished. You couldn't add one more stone because there would be no place to put it, and you couldn't subtract a stone without leaving a hole.

There the pyramid sat, in near geometric, arithmetic, and aesthetic perfection, a precisely articulated construction so big you could fit the Cathedrals of Florence, Milan, St. Paul's in London, Westminster Abbey, *and* St. Peter's in Rome inside it and still have lots of room left over. A structure so perfectly built that it sits almost exactly in line with true north and south or east and west, with each side of the pyramid — two-and-a-half football fields long — almost exactly the same length (there are less than eight inches difference between the longest and the shortest sides). All this was done without power tools, without modern precision instruments, and without the engine. It was hand-made in the true sense of being hand-made, over four thousand years ago, sitting in the flat, empty desert west of the Nile.

Could this pyramid have been buit anywhere else and still

keep its power over the imagination? Could the Great Pyramid have been built in the jungle? Or how about on Manhattan Island? Yes and no. We've seen the pre-Colombian step pyramids of Central America built in the jungle. And we've seen the skyscrapers of New York City that are in their own way modern versions of the pyramid.

The idea of the pyramid isn't exclusive to deserts. But there's something about the connection of pyramid to empty desert that intensifies the effect. It doesn't have to compete with the jungle, which threatens to swallow it the way the jungle overran the pyramids of Central America. And it doesn't have to compete with the crammed colony of other skyscrapers in New York, each detracting from the other. Each pyramid in its own place makes its own statement, and no two are alike. But no pyramid makes a statement nearly as grand, nearly as awe-inspiring as the Great Pyramid of Khufu, standing like a beacon pointing unto heaven.

The lesson of this chapter is two-fold. One: the setting of your work is much more than incidental. It is part of the ecosystem of your work, and to ignore it is to make the other elements of the system suffer. Two: with the addition of setting and the concept of the ecosystem, you can see the various patterns of storytelling begin to converge and integrate into a whole.

It is here that your work becomes more than the simple sum of its parts.

CHAPTER 9

PATTERNS OF STYLE

GRACE UNDER PRESSURE

Style, you say, is an add-on. It's something you worry about if you can find the time to worry about anything beyond the heap of worries you already have. Style is nice if you can manage it, but it isn't all that important.

This attitude is common among beginning writers. The only problem with it is that it's dead wrong.

Somewhere along the way we've separated style from substance. We treat style as if it's a refinement, like adding final touches to the finished product to give it a little something extra. Except that style *is* substance and you can't separate the two. In writing you don't get extra style points as you do in some sports. If your style fails, then the work fails; if the work fails, then you fail. Style is as important a part of the literary ecosystem as plot or character or any of the other parts. The Comte de Buffon said it clearly: "The style is the man himself." I will modify his statement for our discussion: "Style is the work itself."

What is style, then? Is it *flair*, as when we say he has a certain style? Is it a *fashionable elegance*, as when we talk about the clothing styles in this month's issue of *Cosmopolitan* or *GQ*? Is it the scoop of french vanilla ice cream on top of a piece of steaming apple pie, which we call *à la mode*? These are superficial definitions of style, and unfortunately, we're more familiar with these definitions than with the fundamental meaning of style.

Style is language, and language is the artist's medium. We

wouldn't tolerate for a moment a painter who doesn't understand how to use paints. Nor can we tolerate a writer who doesn't understand how to use language. Oh, well, you say, English is the one language I do know.

A famous professor of languages was once interviewed about his talent for foreign languages. He apparently was fluent in about twelve languages, and the interviewer, impressed by his ability, asked, "Professor, how many languages do you really know?" Without missing a beat, the professor answered, "Half of English."

His answer reminds us that none of us *really* know much about even our native language. We speak and write it every day and so we take it for granted. The English language has over 500,000 words in it, and yet the average working vocabulary of the man or the woman on the street is about 5,000 words. That's *1 percent of the total*! Suddenly we feel pretty ignorant. The professor was probably exaggerating when he said he knew *half* of English.

And that's just words. We have to put words together to make sentences. Enter grammar and punctuation. How well do you know grammar? Enough to get by? Get by *what*?

All those rules, you groan. All those exceptions. I've heard students try to claim immunity from prosecution for disobeying the laws of grammar and punctuation with the defense, "What difference does it make as long as I can get my idea across?"

That's the point exactly. How can you get your idea across if you can't express it clearly? "Everything that can be thought at all can be thought clearly," said the philosopher Ludwig Wittgenstein. "Everything that can be said can be said clearly." Norman Mailer put it more directly: "Style is character. A good style cannot come from a bad, undisciplined character." The *way* you write affects *what* you say.

This is a big pill for some to swallow, but the medium *is* the message. In *The Elements of Style*, by E. B. White and William Strunk, White writes: "Every writer, by the way he uses the language, reveals something of his spirit, his habits, his capacities, his bias. This is inevitable as well as enjoyable. . . ."

D. H. Lawrence hated *Moby Dick*. "At first you are put off by the style," he complained. "It reads like journalism. It seems spurious. You feel Melville is trying to put something over you. . . ." (The same complaints have been made against Hemingway.) But then consider this line from *Moby Dick*:

> Now small fowls flew screaming over the yet yawning gulf; a sullen white surf beat against its steep sides; then all collapsed, and the great shroud of the sea rolled on us as it rolled five thousand years ago.

Journalism? Spurious? Not a chance. More like poetry. You can hear the sea in the words and feel it in the swelling rhythm of the sentence itself. Consummate craftsmanship, conveying feeling and meaning through style. Melville does swamp us at times with details about whales and the sea and of sailing; we no longer have the tolerance for that kind of material. We are impatient children who demand to be entertained every minute.

Here's a line from Henry James, considered by critics to be one of the finest American stylists ever:

> Though wasted and shrunken, she still occupied her high-backed chair with a visible theory of erectness, and her intensely aged face — combined with something dauntless that belonged to her very presence and that was effective even in this extremity — might have been that of some immemorial sovereign, of indistinguishable sex, brought forth to be shown to the people in disproof of the rumour of extinction.

Writing like this, though admired by many for its style, prompted others to express their own distaste for that same style. Oscar Wilde made the unflattering comment that James "writes fiction as if it were a painful duty." William Faulkner was cattier when he said "Henry James was one of the nicest old ladies I ever met." Virginia Woolf, Somerset Maugham, H. L. Mencken all had nasty things to say about the writing of Henry James too. Compare the sensual quality of the quote from Melville with the abstract, tinder-dry quality of the quote from James. In terms of crafting, both are superb. The difference is that Melville's writing is wired to the senses, while James' writing is wired to the mind. The Melville quote is more feeling than idea, while the James quote is more idea than feeling. Which is more correct? That depends upon the patterns in your ecosystem. It depends upon your theme. Is it action? (In which case Melville's style would work and James' style wouldn't). Or is it idea? (In which case James' style would clearly work better than Melville's). Style isn't something you arbitrarily plug in; it is a function of your plot, your characters, and your themes.

Note, for example, how Dickens' style is affected by function in this quote from *Bleak House* in which he introduces Mr. Turveydrop:

> He was a fat old gentleman with a false complexion, false teeth, false whiskers, and a wig. . . . He was pinched in, and swelled out, and got up, and strapped down, as much as he could possibly bear. He had such a neckcloth on (puffing his very eyes out of their natural shape), and his chin and even his ears so sunk into it, that he seemed as though he must inevitably double up, if it were cast loose. He had, under his arm, a hat of great size and weight, shelving downward from the crown to the brim; and in his hand a pair of white gloves, with which he flapped it, as he stood poised on one leg, in a high-shouldered, round-elbowed state of elegance not to be surpassed. He had a cane, he had an eye-glass, he had rings, he had wrist-bands, he had everything but any touch of nature; he was not like youth, he was not like age, he was not like anything in the world but a model of Deportment.

Dickens' style conveys the character of the man not only in the details, but in the specific choices of words, in the construction of the sentences and the rhythms they create. It would have been much easier for Dickens to write something like:

> The gentleman was fat and had a bad complexion. He also had false teeth, a fake beard and a wig. . . . He was bulged in some places and was pinched in others. He wore a neckcloth that was so tight his eyes bulged, and his chin

and eyes seemed to disappear so that he seemed twice his actual size. He carried a huge hat and a pair of white gloves under his arm. He flapped the gloves as he stood balanced on one leg. He also had a cane, an eye-glass, and wrist-bands, and rings. Nothing was natural about him. He didn't look either young or old. He looked like a model of Deportment.

The energy of the writing is drained. It lacks the vitality of the original. The sentences are unimaginative, and the descriptions seem more like an inventory of details than the spirited characterization which is the essence of Mr. Turveydrop. Dickens exemplifies Toni Morrison's advice when she said that "language must be careful and must appear effortless. It must not sweat. It must suggest and be provocative at the same time."

Piano Grammar

Joan Didion once called grammar the piano she played by ear. Do you have to learn the tortured maze of English grammar in order to write well? Do you have to know the endless rules and exceptions of do's and don'ts before you can put word to paper? Of course not. Grammar was always a mystery to me in school, as it was for most of us. If we were lucky we learned some basic rules that have stuck with us. We learned to spell reasonably well, and to sense at least when we were getting in over our heads. As you learn to be a writer, you should find yourself interested in the language itself—in words and their power, in grammar and its power. This intrigue is no different than the painter's fascination with oils: What are their properties? How do they work? How do they combine? Or the photographer's fascination with the properties and functions of film. Every art has its own grammar and syntax. The more accomplished the artist, the greater his or her understanding of how far the limits of both can be pushed.

Taking a crash course in grammar probably won't help you much (unless of course you're *so* bad). Most writers I know who have achieved any kind of competency in these areas were self-taught. They learned it from other writers in their works, and they learned it from browsing in the manuals of style and in dictionaries. Style is something you develop over time, not something you can install like a computer program. The Picasso we know didn't start out that way. Nor did Van Gogh or Beethoven or Joyce. They started out like everyone else, painting, composing or writing like anyone else. But with time they found a unique way to express their ideas, a way that was absolutely Van Gogh or Beethoven or Joyce. These artists reached the epitome of style. We don't have to see their names to know their work. How did they learn the grammar and syntax of their respective arts? In school? No. In doing.

I have nothing against the English teachers in this country. They teach what and how they believe they ought to teach, and to some degree, we are all victims of that teaching.

Victims?

I wish somebody had taught me when I was young that language is alive, not something that is dead and pinned to the page in dictionaries. I wish somebody had taught me that grammar was alive and breathing, not a mummified corpse swathed in two thousand years of rules, delivered to us like the Hundred Commandments. It took me years to learn that a dictionary is nothing more than a snapshot of our language—a snapshot that is on the average ten to twenty years old—and the dictionary doesn't exist that can capture the vitality of a language that's always moving, changing, and flexing its muscles. I learned that the books of lessons about grammar are more interested in dictating law than teaching people how to write well. When you see what great writers can do with language, and how they make their own rules of grammar that are as elegant and graceful as anything anyone has ever written, then you know that rules aren't really rules, they're guidelines.

But Picasso was right when he said you have to learn the rules before you can break them. Within rules lies tradition—seven thousand years of it.

Don't make the same mistake Humpty Dumpty made by arbitrarily corrupting rules of language. "When *I* use a word," Humpty Dumpty said, in a rather scornful tone, "it means just what I choose it to mean — neither more nor less." The result is chaos for Humpty Dumpty: hopeless fragments.

Tradition has value and it has wisdom. Your task is to find the value, learn its wisdom, and then learn how to apply it to your own voice and vision as a writer. With time you will begin to hear the music, and with time, the music will become familiar. And as you become comfortable with it, you'll begin to play variations on the themes of language and grammar. This music is your music; it is the creation of your style.

Butter Words

This chapter wouldn't be complete if it didn't include some notions about how to improve your style, and the best place to start is with words.

"Words . . ." wrote John Steinbeck, "pick up flavors and odors like butter in the refrigerator." The English language has both breadth and depth: 500,000 words and sometimes as many as forty and fifty definitions for a word. (Look up the word "point" in your dictionary.) And that's only a fraction of the language that dictionaries can capture. They can't deal with the connotative side of what words suggest. How many words are there with all the connotations and denotations available to them? A billion? Ten billion? Probably more. And the total grows daily.

Every writer is a student of words. We want to break out of the limited five thousand word vocabulary of the average working stiff. We want to explore: by peeking into corners where no one's been for a while, by rooting around in cellars and attics in order to see what lost treasures we can find. We begin to feel the power of language, and language is power in the real sense of the word.

We are each in search of the right word, the word that carries within it not just meaning but the power of feeling, the word that can wrench a gut, threaten or calm, or sing. So, in light of that, I say:

Eschew logorrheic sesquipedalianism.

Fancy words, right? What do fancy words do to you when

you read them? They alienate you. They make you feel stupid if you don't know them (and they make you feel smart if you do). But whom are you writing for? The 2 percent of the population who know what those words mean? Or for the other 98 percent who are angry at you for showing off? What am I saying? Plain English, please.

Anytime a reader trips over a word or words (especially when they're as high-falutin' as "logorrheic sesquipedalianism") the author's trance over the reader is broken. Remember when you last ran into an entirely mystifying word? How did you feel? What did you feel toward the author? Chances are you felt annoyed that you had to deal with a word you didn't know, and then chances are you felt annoyed with the author for stopping you cold like that. We may like to learn new words, but we don't want to have to look them up when we're in the middle of reading. Your train of thought, your rhythm and the rhythm of the story have been interrupted. Why?

As the author, you must answer that question if you use words that few people know. So what does *eschew logorrheic sesquipedalianism* mean? Eschew: avoid. Logorrhea: diarrhea of the mouth. Sesquipedalianism: big, fat words (actually, "words seven feet long"). Translation: Don't use big, weird words. If you do decide to use a big word, then make sure you have a solid reason and that the word's pretty clear in context, without resort to a dictionary. Be practical and be considerate of your readers. After all, as Mark Twain was fond of pointing out, when you're getting paid by the word, why use *metropolis* when you get paid the same for *city*?

Gertrude Stein once complained that words like *love*, and *moon*, and *rose* have lost their power because they've been used so often that we no longer have any real feeling for the words themselves. A writer's job is to bring feeling back into these common words, to stop the reader from gliding over them because they're already too familiar. You can't say the word *love* anymore and expect to generate any significant feeling unless it's in a very personalized context, such as with two lovers. As writers we use the word *love* over and over and over, the same way each time so that it's no wonder readers have become desensitized to it.

We have to find ways to reinvigorate the word, to bring life back to its spiritless body. Simply saying it doesn't make it so anymore.

My point is that we seldom take time to know what words really mean. Not fancy words, but everyday words. We know one or two of their more common meanings and then we ignore the richness of other possibilities.

Writing becomes exciting when you use common words in uncommon ways. Recently I heard a story on the radio that described a scene in which a boy was climbing through a wrought-iron fence. The author could have chosen any number of words to describe how the boy got through the fence. The fit was tight. He could have said, "The boy carefully squeezed himself through the fence." But that makes him sound more like a link of sausage. "The boy wriggled through the fence." Now he sounds like a worm. "Pushed" is flat and uninteresting and "squirmed" brings us back to a worm. None of these words are bad; it's that they've been used in the same way so many times.

Then how did the author describe the action of the boy passing through the fence? "He insinuated himself between the bars of the fence." *Insinuated*. We usually think of the word *insinuated* as meaning "to introduce an idea gradually or in a subtle or indirect way," as in, *He insinuated that I was a liar*. But it also means "to enter gently, slowly, or imperceptibly, to creep." Perfect. We can see the boy gingerly insinuating himself between the wrought-iron bars of the fence and finessing his way through. *Insinuate* is a wonderful choice of a word: it is bright, original, and clear.

If you want to study words, then, study the words you already know. Do not know them superficially; know them for all they're worth.

Life Sentences

In his book *Style*, Joseph Williams writes, "The very act of writing and rewriting helps us clarify our ideas, better understand what we want to say, find the best way to organize our material, and speak to the interests and needs of our readers."

You begin your story with the first word of the first sentence and you end it with the last word of the last sentence. Sentences are patterns of words. They are the essential units of thought. If the sentence doesn't work, then nothing works.

There are whole books devoted to the proper way to write a sentence. (I recommend Williams' book: it's one of the few books written on style that actually has some.) Sentences are the arteries that bring the life's blood of the story to the surface. If those arteries clog; the patient will die.

There are short sentences and long sentences; sentences that compound thoughts and sentences that float like lilies in a pond. The rhythm of action and character is controlled by the rhythm of your sentences. You can alter mood, increase or decrease tension, and pace the action by the number of words you put in a sentence. And because sentences create patterns, then the cumulative effect of your sentences has a larger overall effect on the work itself. Short sentences are more dramatic; long sentences are calmer by nature and tend to be more explanatory or descriptive. If you're writing a tense scene and use long sentences, you may be working against yourself. And if you're writing a relaxed scene that you intend to be peaceful and you use short, choppy sentences, then you could be working against yourself there, too. As you write, make sure your sentences *feel* right. Make sure they carry the emotion you want to convey. Read the Dickens quote above and notice how the long structure creates a sense of character presence rather than just a collection of details. The sentence, although descriptive, increases in complexity and yet manages to still convey the humor that is so typical of Dickens' descriptions. Compare that sentence, with its jumps and starts, with the calmer, flowing sentence from *Moby Dick*, or the labyrinthine sentence from James. Each creates a different effect, and that effect is suited to the character or theme or mood.

The question comes up frequently, "How long should a sentence be?" A sentence is a reflection of dramatic structure. It has a beginning, a middle, and an end: subject, action, finality. The subject acts upon something or is acted upon by something: three parts, Act I, II, and III. Therefore a sentence ought to reflect your larger scale dramatic structure (an example of relationship in your ecosystem).

A sentence can be one word long or it can be a hundred. Too many short sentences eventually create an effect that will annoy the reader: "Frank stood up. He picked up a long stick. He then glared at Bill. Bill looked nervous. Frank took one step toward Bill. Bill stepped back." The sounds of these sentences are creating a monotonous rhythm. Try combining the little sentences into one long sentence: "Frank stood up and picked up a long stick and then stepped toward Bill, which made him so nervous that he stepped back." Is this sentence better? No, because it combines two separate images and an action-response, cause and effect situation that would best be handled with a mix of sentences: "Frank stood, picked up a stick, and stepped toward Bill." (Action/cause) "Bill, nervous, stepped back." (Reaction/effect) The longer first sentence sets up the sharper and more dramatic second.

One last warning. The longer the sentence, the greater the likelihood you will lose your reader. Any sentence over twenty words will tax the attention of your reader. The longer the sentence, the more the reader has to remember, and the more likely he will forget some of those details. That's why writers like Henry James are tough to read: he demands a lot of the reader in every sentence. Reading Marcel Proust is like getting on a subway with no stops: each sentence takes you half way across the city, but Proust makes the ride worth it. Readers do run out of breath when reading a long sentence. If you can read a sentence out loud without gasping for breath, then it's a comfortable length; if you find yourself gulping for air, then the sentence is as taxing on the eye (and mind) as it is on your lungs. Use your long sentences sparingly and for effect. The Melville quote, for instance, needs length to create the sounds of the sea with all the S's and with the long, rolling feel of the sentence. He couldn't have achieved the same effect with a short sentence.

The last piece of advice comes from Hemingway, who struggled long and hard with style. "All you have to do is write one true sentence," he said. "Write the truest sentence that you know."

CHAPTER 10

INTEGRATING THE WHOLE

DEATH IN PITTSBURGH

Willa Cather's short story, "Paul's Case" is a beautifully crafted work, widely recognized by readers and critics as one of her best short works. Even Ms. Cather was partial to it: for years "Paul's Case" was the only story she would allow to be anthologized.

The story is about a teen-aged rebel who can't stand the drab, meaningless existence of middle-class Pittsburgh. Paul has been suspended from Pittsburgh High School for his habitual disorder and impertinence, and when he shows up before the review board to discuss readmission, Paul dresses outrageously, like a character out of a British farce, complete with flaming red carnation in his buttonhole. His inquisitors descend upon him viciously, but Paul is immune, and leaves the school whistling the Soldiers' Chorus from *Faust*.

Paul's passion is the theater where he is an usher and a hanger-on with a stock theater company. The passion and vibrancy and drama of life in the theater consume him. He can find everything life lacks outside the doors of Carnegie Theater inside on the stage, and he basks in its glow as he desperately tries to forget the drab reality that awaits him in life. Outside, in the streets, is hell; inside, on the stage, is heaven.

Hell is Cordelia Street where Paul lives with his father. He hates the merchants, always chasing the almighty dollar; he hates the pictures of John Calvin and George Washington that hang over his bed; he hates the colorless monotony of his life.

Paul is hungry for something else, and nothing in the life around him offers him any possibility of escape from the prison of middle-class. Nothing but the theater.

And then, suddenly and cruelly, circumstances force drastic change. Paul's father takes him out of school on the principal's advice, forbids him to return to the theater, and orders his son to get a job.

Paul is devastated. A quiet, solitary, and introverted person, he can't communicate his feeling to anyone, so he obeys his father and takes a job with a local firm. And one day his employers make the mistake of asking Paul to deposit the day's receipts in the bank.

A thousand dollars. Paul cannot resist the temptation of stealing the money and running away to the home of real theater and culture: New York City. He takes the first train east to New York in search of what he has yearned for all his life: the good life in the magical city, the temple of culture, where people were anything but mundane. Paul checks into the Waldorf Astoria and for a week gorges himself on the pleasures of money and the city.

But the money runs out and Paul is left with nothing except the news that his father has paid back the thousand dollars to the firm and is on his way to fetch Paul.

Paul takes the ferry to Newark and then takes a cab out of town. Leaving the cab, Paul walks aimlessly along the railroad tracks dreading his return to the horrors of Pittsburgh. He realizes he cannot go back, and as a train comes barreling toward him, Paul throws himself onto the tracks, realizing at the last moment that he has made a terrible mistake: that instead of going to New York, he should have gone abroad where the real paradise must certainly lie.

The description in the story is straightforward, and in the paraphrase the real story is lost, of course. Details always make the story. Cather subtitled her story "A Study in Temperament," which clues us as to the work's theme: character. We know from the title that this is "Paul's Case," and that we are to examine him the way a sociologist might study a case in point. And "Paul's Case" is a sad case.

As you create your characters, give them every chance to come alive by creating the right environment for them to play out their action. The environment I'm talking about isn't limited to just a place, but includes all the patterns of structure, plot, action, character, theme, place, and style. In "Paul's Case" Cather creates this environment in several important ways, each of which relies on the others for its success. None of the patterns of the narrative really work independently; they work together, in concert, becoming greater than the sum of their parts.

The effect of integration isn't something you can control entirely. When it works well, it works wonderfully, creating an undefinable magic. Everything comes together, usually in ways you could never anticipate. Patterns don't compete; they unify. We say the work takes on a life of its own.

And when it works poorly, it works very poorly, creating an unmitigated disaster. The plot won't jell, the characters won't jell, the story doesn't hum, it sputters. The whole is nothing more than the sum of its individual parts, each independent of the other.

"Paul's Case" integrates the various patterns of technique ranging from plot to place. These aren't separate patterns; they're the same pattern repeated and reinforced by technique. By looking at how these various patterns merge in "Paul's Case," we can see how the artist adapts the patterns of technique so that they mesh. In the early drafts of your work there are bound to be very many jagged edges. Patterns don't always mesh well at first. First draft is raw ore that must be refined through the process of rewriting. And rewriting means first discovering the nature of the work as it now exists on the page (as compared to what you thought you were going to write way back when), and then reshaping the work to make the pieces fit snugly so that the seams between techniques disappear and the picture suddenly unifies. It's an exciting process because as a writer you see the real nature of your work start to emerge in much the same way as a butterfly emerges from its case.

By tracing the patterns of technique in "Paul's Case," I hope to give a glimpse of the process of making the patterns merge by the process of rewriting. This is speculative, of course, and I can't really hope to guess what was on Ms. Cather's mind at any given moment, but the decisions she made, either consciously or subconsciously, were the right decisions to unify the major patterns of the work.

PATTERN OF STRUCTURE

The dramatic pattern of the story has the traditional three movement structure. The first movement (set-up) takes place in Pittsburgh and picks up with Paul having been suspended from school and petitioning for readmission. It continues through to the first crisis point of the story, when his father takes him out of school and makes him get a job.

The second movement (complications) begins when Paul decides to take the money and run away to New York, and continues through to the second crisis point of the story, when he learns his father has repaid the money and is coming to get him.

The third movement (resolution) begins when Paul takes the ferry to Newark and ends with the climax, when he throws himself in front of the train.

Beauty in simplicity. Cather follows the pattern carefully and keeps the movements in balance. She doesn't explain too much in setting up Paul's Case — she starts the story as late as possible (with Paul in trouble at school which leads directly to his father taking him out). The movements within the structure are separated by clearly defined crisis points which force change to take place. Which leads us directly to the pattern of action. . . .

PATTERN OF ACTION

The action is closely suited to the structure of the story and its plot. Read the story and you'll see clearly that Cather only put into the story what was necessary for the story to happen. The events never wander; their path is straight and narrow through the plot (which is discussed in the next section).

The first movement opens up with Paul before the school review board. We learn that his teachers don't like him because he isn't like the other schoolchildren. This idea is reinforced by the outrageous way Paul dresses and his apparent lack of concern for what the teachers have to say to him. Paul leaves the review and goes directly to the theater, which is his escape. And from the theater he goes home to Cordelia Street. The first three action sequences of the story are designed to give us the three places that make up Paul's world and show us how he acts in each: school, the theater, and at home. There are no scenes and no action to detract from our understanding of Paul's closed world.

The second movement starts with Paul fleeing what he perceives to be his prison. The action is definite: stealing his employer's money and running away to New York. The action in New York is just as definite. He checks into the Waldorf and begins to enjoy the life he believes he was meant to enjoy. Paul buys himself nice clothes, fills his room with masses of flowers, eats huge meals, and sleeps late. He goes to the theater. Everything he does reveals something to us about who he really is and what is happening to his dream. More so than in the first movement, Paul's actions in the second movement reveal more about the true nature of his character. If the first movement was the nightmare (Pittsburgh) and the dream (the theater), then the second movement is the dream (New York) turned into reality which, in the third movement, becomes the nightmare. The motion is circular: nightmare – dream – nightmare – dream – nightmare. Each time the nightmare returns, Paul finds a way to escape it. And what Paul does makes that circle of events happen. Notice this isn't a story about what *happens* to Paul but what Paul does himself. He is his own victim, not the victim of an indifferent or cruel world.

The action of the third movement is clearest of all: when Paul reads in the Pittsburgh paper that his father has paid back the thousand dollars and is on his way to New York, he must react. His options are limited. He can't run because the money is gone. He can't go back to Pittsburgh now that he's tasted the dream. The nightmare reappears and offers him no way out, and so he does what he believes is his only choice: he kills himself. Now the nightmare has no chance of exit, and he ends up in a hell far worse than the one he imagined he was in while living in Pittsburgh.

Every act of Paul follows the path of nightmare-dream-nightmare. The action is to the point, stripped of everything that doesn't accomplish this end. No side trips. The author knows what she wants to accomplish (through the patterns of plot and theme) and has adapted the action (through rewriting) to make it happen. Paul moves from prisoner (in Pittsburgh) to escape (mentally, by escaping to the Carnegie Theater), to recapture (mentally, when his father takes him out of school and forbids him to return to the theater), to another escape (this time physical, when he steals the money and runs away), to recapture again (physically, when his father comes to get him), to escape (the final kind, through suicide), which, of course, is his final recapture. The prisoner, seeking permanent freedom, finds only permanent imprisonment.

PATTERN OF PLOT

The plot pattern for "Paul's Case" is *Obtaining*. In this pattern, the protagonist has some goal he wants to achieve and then strives to achieve it, either successfully or unsuccessfully. This plot pattern fits perfectly with the pattern of action. Paul wants escape and does what he has to in order to get away and lose himself in the dream. The three dramatic phases of the plot pattern lend themselves to the pattern of action. First, the main character must desire something. Paul desires escape. Second, the main character must make an attempt to achieve that something. Paul does, twice. First symbolically by working in the theater, and the second time when he runs away to New York. Third, the main character must either succeed or fail at obtaining his goal. Paul seems to succeed at first but of course he fails. Each of the three dramatic phases overlaps exactly with the pattern of structure (in its three movements) and with the pattern of action.

THE PATTERN OF CHARACTER

The focus of the story is Paul. We see and hear everything through Paul. No other characters really seem to exist in the story. Cather virtually eliminates any other characters in the story so that Paul is the only person in focus at any given time. The teachers at Pittsburgh High, Paul's father, and everyone else appear only fleetingly, like shadows that barely touch Paul's life. Notice how this strengthens the story, because Paul is isolated from everyone else. He communicates poorly with others, partly because he doesn't want to reach out to other people and partly because he doesn't know how. Paul is stranded on an island, and his loneliness fires his imagination about another place where he could be happy. It makes perfect sense, then, that all the people that Paul should come into contact with should be sketchy because that's exactly how Paul relates to other people.

If you look at the total number of lines of dialogue in the story, you'll realize how little there is. Why? Because Paul can't communicate with other people, and when he does say something to the other characters, it too is alienated. We judge Paul by his action (which takes us back to the pattern of action). Even the nature of the plot pattern makes us examine the main character carefully. We are forced to ask the question, "What does Paul want?" And when we learn what his dream is, we then ask, "How will he get it?" The rest of the story is devoted to answering that question, but in ways we couldn't have predicted.

PATTERN OF THEME

We can't talk about character without talking about theme. What Paul doesn't understand is that the ideals of Cordelia Street, with its white collar workers and their wives who attend ice cream socials at church, are really his own ideals. Paul's vision of the world is distorted. He distorts the operas and plays he sees, he distorts the lives of the actors he works with, he distorts the world of art. He believes he isn't suited to the world of Cordelia Street with its emphasis on making money and moving up in the world; rather, he thinks he's meant for the world of art. But what does Paul do when he steals the money? He gorges himself. In New York he only goes to the theater *once*; he spends the rest of the time eating, sleeping, and spending money. Paul has no talent and no ambition; he's just as unsuited for the world of art as he is in his real life. Paul doesn't have the ability to weigh alternatives or consequences; he has no will to resist. He's alienated from all worlds except the world of fantasy which leads him to his death. Paul seeks escape, but from what and to what? He doesn't really know. He thinks from the world of grubby capitalism into the sacred world of art which is free from the dirt of the world. But when his chance comes, he is more interested in wealth than in art. Paul has been lured into a false garden, a distorted garden of his own imagination, which of course life cannot provide. What Paul never understands is that he loves not art, but dazzle.

The theme is the relationship of dream to nightmare and the relationship between capture and escape. Be careful what you dream for, Cather seems to be warning, you might get it. This pattern of thinking is consistent with all the other patterns; they rely on the theme to make sense, and the theme relies on them to make sense.

PATTERN OF PLACE

Pittsburgh is dark and grimy and suffocating through Paul's eyes. Cordelia Street is worse. He hates his home with its grimy zinc tub and cracked mirrors and ugly yellow wallpaper. He hates his father's hairy legs and carpet slippers. But when Paul is in the theater, everything is colorful and full of life. The comparison is easy: ugly against beautiful, at least as Paul sees it, which helps build the patterns of character and theme. The same is true in New York, which is described as a garden of earthly delights, an Eden for the imagination. But Paul closes himself off even in New York. He shuts himself in his room, surrounds himself with an artificial garden of cut flowers, and floats off into a death-like trance. Cather then contrasts the glittering world of New York with the drabness of Newark, where Paul meets his death on the cold, black tracks. Each of these places is critical to the story. Pittsburgh, New York, and Newark. Each one represents either the dream or the nightmare. Cather's descriptions of each make them functions of the story.

PATTERN OF STYLE

Because Paul is alienated, Cather makes sure we don't get too close to him so that we feel for him. She wants us to look at him from the distance so we can better understand the theme of the work. She wants us to concentrate on Paul's self-destructive nature and not get caught up in his glitzy vision of the world of art. She doesn't want Paul's fantasy to seduce us. To do that, she uses a style that keeps a distance between us and Paul. We always see Paul from a distance. We know what he thinks, but it's presented to us almost clinically, suggested by the subtitle of the work, "A Study in Temperament." The author doesn't want us to be seduced the way Paul has been seduced, and so she must make us keep our distance and regard him coldly so we can learn the lesson that Paul can't learn.

Cather constructs a series of patterns that rely upon each other in order to create the various tensions of the work. These patterns combine to create an ecosystem, in which each component contributes to the whole. As you write, as you create the patterns of your work, you should try to make your choices in such a way that the individual patterns become stronger when they join the other major patterns you've created. One pattern shouldn't work against another. You can't even afford a neutral pattern, because even a neutral pattern (one which neither adds nor detracts from the other patterns) becomes a lost chance, an uninspired blankness in your work which will cause your story to lose its force.

DECISION TIME

You've no doubt figured out by now that stories don't just fall into place; you must make them fit, the same way a cabinetmaker must be skilled in joinery. Writing is a long process of making choices. Thousands of choices. Word by word, image by image, scene by scene from beginning to end and back to the beginning again.

The more aware you are of the choices you have to make the better your decisions will be. A writer can't afford to ignore the decisions that have to be made by blindly forging ahead and hoping for the best. Every decision you make—about plot, action, character, and theme—will affect the ecosystem of your work. A bad decision will take you off the track, and the work will wander, until eventually both you and the work will be hopelessly lost.

The diagram below represents, in a crude way, the interrelationships between the various systems in a literary ecosystem. Use this diagram as a test to apply to your developing concept of a story. Following the diagram are the critical questions every writer must ask in the course of writing his or her story. It should help you focus on the basic patterns you need to develop in order to pull together the various elements of fiction into a single, meaningful whole.

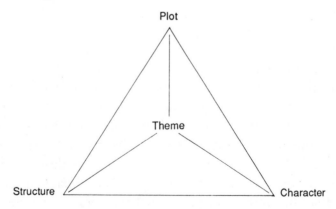

Ask yourself the eight questions listed below. Not to have an answer, or at least an idea of an answer, can stymie your best efforts. Don't ignore any of these questions; if you do, they'll come back to haunt you, like one of Paul's nightmares.

They are:

1. What plot pattern would best suit the story you want to tell? (Chapter Four)
2. What are the dramatic phases of the plot pattern you've chosen for your work? (Chapter Four)
3. How can you translate the dramatic phases into specific actions for your characters? (Chapter Five)
4. What kind of structure would best suit the action? (Chapter Three)
5. What (and how many) characters would best fit the plot? (Chapter Six)
6. What kind of focus (theme) do you want to bring to your story? How will that focus affect the plot and the characters? (Chapter Seven)
7. What kind of setting would best fit the characters and the action of the plot? (Chapter Eight)
8. What writing style would best suit the story? (Chapter Nine)

If you can answer these questions with reasonable certainty, and be willing to keep an open mind if opportunity knocks, then you'll have established for yourself three of the most critical elements for successful writing: a foundation that is solid, a direction to pursue, and a plan to follow.

You can't avoid these decisions, because every page you write deals with them even if by default. You'll know soon enough if your decisions are right or wrong, but take a stand. Forcing yourself to deal with the central issues of your work makes you think through the work and focus on its important elements.

Remember also that a certain amount of flexibility is important for a work to "live" and "breathe." If you have plans for one of your characters to go home after work and eat a pot pie, and the character decides instead he'd rather go drinking at the corner bar and play some pinball, you should let your character do what he wants. Don't be a tyrant. Sometimes characters willingly do what you plan for them to do, and sometimes they'll fight you tooth and nail to do something else, something unpredictable. And if what they want to do threatens your plan, then maybe the plan is wrong. Or more likely the plan is right, it's just that the characters prefer to do it their own way, which, from all the writers I've ever talked to, is the better way. Every good work has its unexpected turns and twists *for the writer*. It's a good sign, so don't squelch the spontaneous thoughts, actions, and words of your characters. In the long run they can write a better story than you or I ever can. But they do need some guidance, rather like the way a tolerant parent allows the child headroom, but always within constraints.

A PARTING SHOT

Whether you're writing for a commercial market or writing simply to write the best story you know how, you should be serious about your art. The concept of patterns and strategy sometimes suggests that writing is little more than a series of formulas, and if you're good at hitching together formulas, then you can write any kind of book you want. Not true. Patterns and the strategies of how best to create them make, at most, the skeleton of a work, and all works stripped of flesh look pretty much alike as skeletons. What makes a work unique is how you flesh out these patterns. What makes a work imaginative and interesting to others is the details, the shadings, and the shadows.

Earlier in the book I talked about method and madness. Method is technique: you can learn the rules, follow the numbers, practice the skills. Madness, however, deals with the author's vision and voice. Literature succeeds not because it presents new ideas, but because it presents new ways of looking at those ideas. What intrigues us is the way an author "clothes" ideas. What intrigues us is the accent, the stress, the sound of the song itself. All people share pretty much a common experience, and yet each of us sees the world in a slightly different way; we hear and feel the world in a different way; we know it differently too. The art of an author is to convey to others the specialness of how we experience the way of the world, and the people and the places in it.

There are no lessons for teaching madness, that part of us we call "inspired." Some people claim this is the foundation of talent: the ability to convey to others our vision of the world in a voice that is distinctly our own. Yet we are *all* capable of inspiration. Sometimes that vision and voice comes easily for us, while at other times we sit for hours on end in front of a blank page praying for a simple sentence. One thing is true, however: the greater your investment of time and thought in the work, the greater the work will be. If you're in a hurry, and if you try to rush through your decisions and cut corners on technique, you can't expect anything as complex as a story to come to complete term.

Writing is an act of love, and like any relationship of substance, you should be willing to make a commitment to work and to time so that it can mature. And despite the seemingly endless tangle of frustrations and disappointments, despite the daily struggle to find the right word and the right action, and despite all those moments of doubt when you're not sure if all the months (or even years) of hard labor you've plunked down are really worth it, suddenly one day the story comes together with all the intricacy of the kaleidoscopic image, pattern merging with pattern, so that all the bits and pieces become a single, beautiful design unified on the page and in your mind. That moment is worth all the suffering it took to get there, and more.

This is the moment of illumination, the moment when the clouds that have hovered over everything since the first page and muddled your line of sight suddenly lift and let you see your story clearly from beginning to end. That's the point to which all of us strive in our work, and it's the belief (or the hope) that we will get there eventually that keeps us going.

There are no guarantees, of course; all we have is our ambition, our respect for our abilities, and our love for the story and for work. Without those, we don't have a chance, but with them, the possibilities are endless.

APPENDIX

Plot Patterns

The following plot patterns include not only the basic situations but also the characters that typically play in these situations. This list abbreviates the work of others who have spent much more time cataloging the various shades of each of the plots. My intent here is only to give you the types of plot and the major players in each so you can understand how compact the concept of plot is, and how specific the patterns are to each. If you want to read more, I recommend Georges Polti's book, *The Thirty-Six Dramatic Situations*, from which these patterns have been condensed.

Plot 1: SUPPLICATION
Major Players: The Persecutor, The Suppliant, A Power in Authority (whose decision is in doubt)

Basic Scenarios: Fugitives Begging a Powerful Figure for Help Against Their Enemies; Appeals for Refuge; Seeking Pardon or Deliverance from Sin.

Notes: A popular plot with the Greeks (Aeschylus, Sophocles, and Euripides, for example), this pattern has fallen from favor because the plot is too simple for our complex tastes.

Plot 2: DELIVERANCE
Major Players: The Unfortunate, The Threatener, The Rescuer

Basic Scenarios: Appearance of a Rescuer to the Condemned; Rescue by Friends or by Strangers.

Notes: We recognize this pattern with Lancelot's deliverance by the Lady of the Lake, just as we recognize the deliverance of many ladies in distress by gallant knights. A staple plot in romance novels. Also popular lately in films that have heroes going back to Vietnam to deliver POWs, such as *Iron Eagle* and Chuck Norris' series of films, *Missing in Action*.

Plot 3: REVENGE

Major Players: The Avenger, The Criminal

Basic Scenarios: Avenging Someone Slain; Avenging Dishonor; Avenging Intentional Injury; the Professional Pursuit of Criminals.

Notes: One of the most popular and enduring of all plots and one of the most powerful emotionally. Discussed in Chapter Four.

Plot 4: VENGEANCE BY FAMILY UPON FAMILY

Major Players: The Avenging Kinsman, The Guilty Kinsman, A Relative of Both.

Basic Scenarios: Avenging the Death or Dishonor of a Family Member by Another Family Member; for instance, a Son Avenges His Father's Murder by His Mother.

Notes: More common in Greek tragedy than in contemporary literature. The story of the house of Atreus is perhaps the most famous example, as it includes generations of revenge by one family member upon another.

Plot 5: PURSUIT

Major Player: The Fugitive Threatened with Capture and Punishment

Basic Scenarios: Fugitive from Justice, Justly or Unjustly; Hero Struggling Against a Power.

Notes: We are more intrigued by characters who are falsely accused than those who are justly pursued. Discussed in Chapter Four.

Plot 6: VICTIM OF CRUELTY OR MISFORTUNE

Major Players: The Unfortunate, a Master or a Misfortunate

Basic Scenarios: The Innocent Made Victim of Ambitious Intrigue; The Innocent Victimized by the Powerful; the Powerful Dispossessed; the Lover Spurned or Forgotten; the Unfortunate Robbed of Hope.

Notes: As Georges Polti writes: "And how many cases yet remain! The Jews in captivity, slavery in America, the Horrors of the Hundred Years' War, invaded ghettoes, scenes such as draw the crowd to any reproduction of prison life or of Inquisition, the attraction of Dante's Inferno. . . ." Injustice makes us bristle, and so the plot is charged emotionally. Vindication is catharsis.

Plot 7: DISASTER

Major Players: The Vanquished Power, the Victorious Enemy or a Messenger

Basic Scenarios: Defeat Suffered; Homeland Destroyed; Threat of the Destruction of Humanity; Natural Catastrophe; Overthrown or Assassinated Ruler; Ingratitude Suffered; Suffering Unjust Punishment; Suffering an Outrage; Abandonment (by lover or a spouse or by parents, intentional or unintentional).

Notes: Catastrophe intrigues us. Popular literature and film is filled with it, and after revenge it is one of the most popular patterns. Science fiction and horror writers favor this pattern. Witness all the stories about nature and technology run amok. Robin Cook (*Coma, Virus*) and Stephen King (*Cujo, Christine*) and Irwin Allen (*Earthquake* and *The Towering Inferno*) are examples.

Plot 8: REVOLT

Major Players: The Tyrant, The Conspirator

Basic Scenarios: Conspiracy; Revolt

Notes: More common than it first seems, the pattern of revolt appears more at an intimate level than at a national or international political level. The rebellion of a child within a family or the rebellion of an individual against society. In some measure *Crime and Punishment* represents Raskolnikov's rebelling against the norms of society. So does Emma Bovary's revolt against provincial life in *Madame Bovary*. In popular literature conspiracy is the mainstay of espionage writers such as Robert Ludlum and Richard Condon. Readers enjoy political intrigue, which is often a prelude to, but usually falls short of the plot pattern DISASTER. Other examples: *Animal Farm, The Caine Mutiny*.

Plot 9: DARING ENTERPRISE

Major Players: The Bold Leader, an Object (Goal), an Adversary

Basic Scenarios: Preparations for War; War; Theft; Recapture of a Desired Object; Adventurous Expeditions; Adventure Undertaken for the Purpose of Obtaining a Beloved.

Notes: The object here may be living or inanimate (such as a treasure). Polti includes "the poetry of war, of robbery, of surprise, of desperate chance," etc. Examples include *The African Queen*, and *Treasure of the Sierra Madre* and nearly any adventure novel you care to mention.

Plot 10: ABDUCTION

Major Players: The Abductor, the Abducted, the Guardian

Basic Scenarios: Kidnapping; Rescue of a Captive

Notes: When Paris kidnapped Helen and carried her off to Troy in the *Iliad*, all hell broke loose. (To complicate matters, both were married, too.) The story has been told many times since, in Euripides's *The Trojan Women*, in Marlowe's *Doctor Faustus* and in Jean Giradoux' *Tiger at the Gates*. The victim doesn't have to be a woman, such as in the case of political kidnapping, hostage taking, or terrorism. An interesting twist on the theme of abduction is in *Extremities*, in which a woman turns the tables on her rapist. Even Jack London's *Call of the Wild* is about the abduction of a dog, Buck, who's pressed into service as a sled dog in the Yukon.

Plot 11: THE ENIGMA

Major Players: The Interrogator, the Seeker, the Problem

Basic Scenarios: Search for a Person or Thing that Must Be Found; A Riddle to Be Solved; Tests that Must Be Passed

Notes: This is the essence of mystery, and as such, it is the primary pattern for mystery and detective novels. The works of Agatha Christie (Hercule Poirot, Miss Marple), Arthur Conan Doyle (Sherlock Holmes), Edgar Allan Poe (C. Auguste Dupin in "The Murders in the Rue Morgue" and "The Purloined Letter") all fall into this category.

Plot 12: OBTAINING

Major Players: A Solicitor, an Adversary Who Refuses to Comply, or an Arbitrator and Opposing Parties

Basic Scenarios: Efforts to Obtain an Object by Ruse or Force; Endeavor by Means of Persuasive Eloquence

Notes: An end to be attained, an object to be gained. Often the hero accomplishes this through diplomacy and eloquence (as opposed to theft or force). Polti has this interesting and slightly sexist comment: "The irritated adversary is here the Defiant; the Solicitor, now the Tempter, has undertaken an unusual negotiation, one for the obtaining of an object which nothing can persuade the owner to part with: consequently the aim must be, gently, little by little, to bewilder, charm or stupefy him. Eternal role of woman toward man!" There are other common uses of this pattern, such as the Devil's clever arguments to gain souls. Obtaining is a common pattern to fairy tales as well, when the hero is put to the test by having to obtain some impossible prize or treasure.

Plot 13: FAMILIAL HATRED

Major Players: Two Family Members Who Hate Each Other

Basic Scenarios: All variations of hatred between family members are possible: Father-Son, Father-Daughter, Husband-Wife, Brother-Brother, Brother-Sister, etc.

Notes: Like Plot 4 (VENGEANCE BY FAMILY UPON FAMILY) the emotions involved between family members are deeper and more explosive. The difficulty with this pattern is to develop a situation emotionally powerful and destructive enough to break the strongest of human ties. In literature and film, the difficulty between generations is often the cause of such a rift, particularly between parents and their children.

Plot 14: FAMILIAL RIVALRY

Major Players: The Preferred Kinsman, the Rejected Kinsman, the Object

Basic Scenarios: Malicious Rivalry between Brothers, Sisters, Father and Son, Mother and Daughter, Cousins, Friends, etc.

Notes: The Object here is often the Beloved. Competition for love and the conflict created by that competition are the powerful emotional forces at play in this pattern. Dostoyevsky's greatest work, *The Brothers Karamazov*, starts off about the rivalry between the father and his son as they compete for the affections of the beautiful Grushenka. Their rivalry leads to the father's murder. Another example, "The Knight's Tale" from the *Canterbury Tales*.

Plot 15: MURDEROUS ADULTERY

Major Players: Two Adulterers, the Betrayed
  Basic Scenario: The Murder of a Spouse or Lover
  Discussed in Chapter Four.

Plot 16: MADNESS

Major Players: The Madman, the Victim
  Basic Scenarios: Family Member or Lover Slain in Madness; Slaying of a Person not Hated; Disgrace through Madness; Loss of Loved Ones
  Notes: The Madness may be divine, demoniac, or pathological, either the result of heredity or the result of artificial causes such as drugs or alcohol. In the twentieth century this plot seems particularly popular as a result of the unprecedented stress we live with. The madness doesn't have to be the raving lunatic type: it can be a quieter, more transient madness that is symptomatic of the ills of our civilization. We recognize this pattern most easily in modern short stories about drug or alcohol abuse and its effect on the individual and his family. Today the concept of madness goes much deeper. In the past madness was an aberration of one; today, we are more likely to view it as an aberration of the whole; that is, society at large. This pattern was popular with Shakespeare too: Lady Macbeth, Hamlet, Timon, Othello, and Lear are all deranged to some extent. Other examples: *Bright Lights, Big City* and *Less Than Zero*.

Plot 17: FATAL IMPRUDENCE

Major Players: The Imprudent, the Victim or the Object Lost

Basic Scenarios: Misfortune to Self or Others as the Result of Carelessness or Imprudence; Misfortune as the Result of Curiosity

Notes: The carelessness usually results by ignoring a law, common sense or other prohibition, and as a result causes harm to self or others. The carelessness might be the result of recklessness, neglect, curiosity, or thoughtlessness. The story of Pandora's box is a classic model. So are many fairy tales in which a character is told not to do something but does it anyway, usually with drastic consequences.

Plot 18: INVOLUNTARY CRIMES OF LOVE

Major Players: The Lover, the Beloved, the Revealer

Basic Scenarios: Unknowing Adultery or Incest

Notes: The story of Oedipus, the man who kills his father and marries his mother. Written by Aeschylus, Sophocles, Seneca, Voltaire, Corneille, and a dozen other authors, including Jean Cocteau's *The Infernal Machine*.

Plot 19: KINSMAN KILLS UNRECOGNIZED KINSMAN

Major Players: The Killer, the Unrecognized Victim (a member of the killer's family)

Basic Scenario: Killing a Family Member by Accident; by Order of a Divinity or Demon; for Political Necessity; as the Result of Rivalry.

Notes: Discussed in Chapter Four.

Plot 20: SELF-SACRIFICE FOR AN IDEAL

Major Players: The Hero, the Ideal, the Person or Thing Sacrificed

Basic Scenario: Sacrificing One's Self for the Sake of Honor, Faith, for Love, Duty or Loyalty

Plot 21: SELF-SACRIFICE FOR KINDRED

Major Players: The Hero, the Kinsman, the Person or Thing Sacrificed

Basic Scenario: Life (or Something of Value) Sacrificed for a Relative.

Notes: Mothers sacrifice themselves for their children (literally and figuratively); husbands for their wives and wives for the husbands; lovers for each other; even faithful animals for their masters. Examples, Shakespeare's *Measure for Measure* and the fairy tale, *Beauty and the Beast*.

Plot 22: ALL SACRIFICED FOR PASSION

Major Players: The Lover, the Object of the Fatal Passion, the Person or Thing Sacrificed

Basic Scenarios: The Ruin of Fortunes, Lives, or Honor As the Result of Being Consumed by any Passion or Vice

Notes: The man (or woman) who gives up all for love. Marc Antony gives up control of Rome for Cleopatra. Samson's passion for Delilah costs him his strength. The passion doesn't have to be erotic. Any obsession, neurotic or psychotic, qualifies. This includes stories involving drug dependencies. The darker side of human nature.

Plot 23: SACRIFICE OF LOVED ONES

Major Players: The Hero, the Beloved Victim, the Necessity for the Sacrifice

Basic Scenario: Sacrificing a Member of the Family, a Lover, or a Friend for What Is Perceived to Be a Greater Good.

Notes: Abraham's willingness to sacrifice Isaac as a burnt offering. Often pits family against obedience to a greater power (either political or divine).

Plot 24: RIVALRY BETWEEN SUPERIOR AND INFERIOR

Major Players: The Superior Rival, the Inferior Rival, the Object

Basic Scenario: The possibilities are endless, ranging from the conflicts between Gods and Men, Rulers and Subjects, and between People (Poor and Rich, Employer and Employed, Parent and Child, Victor and Vanquished, the Powerful and the Powerless, etc.)

Notes: The rivals compete for an object that may be human

(as in the case of suitors), abstract (as in the case of a competition for a job), or inanimate (as in the case of a treasure).

Plot 25: ADULTERY

Major Players: A Deceived Spouse, two Adulterers

   Basic Scenarios: Betrayal; Debauchery; Bigamy; Revenge; Jealousy; Rivalry; etc.

   Discussed in Chapter Four.

Plot 26: CRIMES OF LOVE

Major Players: The Lover, the Beloved

   Basic Scenarios: One Family Member in Love with Another; Bestiality; Incest; Pederasty; Child Abuse; Wife or Husband Abuse

   Notes: This pattern is reserved for specific tragic crimes within the family. Greek and Roman mythology is full of incest and bestiality (Leda and the Swan, Europa and the Bull, etc.), but our focus has changed. In this era of psychorealism, we are more concerned with the crimes committed within the family such as abuse rather than with the fantasies of oversexed gods taking the various shapes of animals.

Plot 27: DISCOVERY OF THE DISHONOR
OF A LOVED ONE

Major Players: The Discovered, the Guilty One

   Basic Scenario: Discovery of a Dark Secret

   Notes: Popular literature favors this pattern. Stories found in romance and detective magazines like to expose the secrets of characters in order to put love or truth to the test. This is the essence of gossip: to lay bare the skeleton in the closet. The point isn't sensationalism, but the crisis created by a truth that a loved one is in fact something other than what was first perceived. A child finds out his father was a convict, a husband finds out his wife was once a prostitute, etc.

Plot 28: OBSTACLES TO LOVE

Major Players: Two lovers, an Obstacle

Basic Scenarios: Marriage Prevented by Inequality of Rank or by Social or Economic Status

Notes: The pattern of "Cinderella," and *The Hunchback of Notre Dame*. We like to believe in the democracy of love: that any two people can fall in love no matter what conditions prohibit success; hence the belief that love conquers all. But the world presents some very real obstacles which in turn create very real conflict. Who will forget that Edward VIII abdicated the throne of England for Wallis Simpson?

Plot 29: AN ENEMY LOVED

Major Players: The Beloved Enemy, the Lover, the Hater

Basic Scenario: Two Lovers Thwarted by Familial Hatred

Notes: *Romeo and Juliet*, of course. The Hatfields and the McCoys. Jean Anouilh's bitter, brutal version of Romeo and Juliet, *Romeo and Jeanette*.

Plot 30: AMBITION

Major Players: An Ambitious Person, a Thing Coveted, an Adversary

Basic Scenario: The Burning Desire for Rank, Power, or Fame

Notes: This pattern examines the aggressive side of the human spirit. Shakespeare was attracted to it in *Julius Caesar*, *Macbeth*, and *Richard III*. Contemporary filmgoers recognize the pattern in *Wall Street*.

Plot 31: CONFLICT WITH A GOD

Major Players: A Mortal, an Immortal

Basic Scenario: Conflict, usually in the form of a Struggle or Challenge between a Mortal and a God

Notes: Odysseus struggled against the gods throughout the *Odyssey*, as do many other mortals, such as Jason, Perseus, and Atreus. The theme of conflict didn't die with the end of classical literature; the struggle became internal rather than external. The story of Job, for example, wherein the Lord, believing in the strength of Job's faith, allows Satan to test him. In spite of

Job's wife's advice to "curse God and die," Job suffers his torment and is rewarded for his steadfastness.

Plot 32: MISTAKEN JEALOUSY

Major Players: The Jealous One, the Object of Whose Possession He Is Jealous, the Supposed Accomplice, the Cause or the Author of the Mistake

Basic Scenarios: Jealousy the Result of Suspicion, Paranoia, Fear of Loss, or the Result of the Deviousness of a Rival or Detractor

Notes: Shakespeare's *Comedy of Errors*. This pattern is often used to comic effect as much as tragic.

Plot 33: FAULTY JUDGMENT

Major Players: The Mistaken One, the Victim of the Mistake, the Cause or Author of the Mistake, the Guilty Person

Basic Scenarios: Plots of Suspicion (of either the Guilty or the Innocent), Indifference, Paranoia, generated by Accident or by Design (by an enemy or rival, for instance).

Notes: Although *King Lear* is about madness, it is also about faulty judgment. Lear misjudges his daughters in the first act when he decides to divide his kingdom among them in return for their declaration of love. Two sisters launch into grandiloquent but hollow speeches praising their father in order to get their share of the take, but Cordelia, Lear's one sincere daughter, refuses to play the game. Lear misjudges her sincerity and his other daughters' hypocrisy. These misjudgments propel Lear to madness and Cordelia to her death.

Plot 34: REMORSE

Major Players: The Culprit, the Victim, the Interrogator

Major Scenarios: Remorse for a Crime, Real or Imagined, Committed with or without Intention, or Intended but not Committed

Discussed in Chapter Four.

Plot 35: RECOVERY OF A LOST ONE

Major Players: The Seeker, the One Found

Basic Scenario: The Return of One Thought Lost or Dead with the Principal Theme of Being Reunited

Notes: The return of Odysseus to his wife Penelope, stories of stolen or switched children, foundlings (popular in fairy tales), falsely imprisoned men (*The Man in the Iron Mask, Richard the Lion-Hearted*), return of the prodigal son. Shakespeare's *Pericles* and *A Winter's Tale*.

Plot 36: LOSS OF LOVED ONES

Major Players: A Kinsman Slain, a Kinsman Witness, an Executioner

Basic Scenario: Suffering Directly or Indirectly the Death of a Loved One

Notes: Our emotions are rarely so easily manipulated as they are in this pattern, and so it is popular in contemporary commercial literature. Many violent "B" films have been made with the loss of a loved one at its focus. A child witnesses the callous murder of a parent; a man witnesses the murder of his wife (or the reverse). How many Westerns have featured savage Indians wiping out wagon trains or settlements save for a witness. The witness will often turn to revenge, but the focus of this pattern isn't retributive action, but the psychological effects of losing a loved one.

Thirty-six patterns. They contain the complete imagination of humanity since the beginning of recorded literature.

INDEX

Other Books of Interest

Annual Market Books

   Artist's Market, edited by Susan Conner $19.95

   Children's Writer's & Illustrator's Market, edited by Connie Eidenier (paper) $14.95

   Novel & Short Story Writer's Market, edited by Laurie Henry (paper) $17.95

   Photographer's Market, edited by Sam Marshall $19.95

   Poet's Market, by Judson Jerome $18.95

   Songwriter's Market, edited by Mark Garvey $18.95

   Writer's Market, edited by Glenda Neff $23.95

General Writing Books

   Annable's Treasury of Literary Teasers, by H.D. Annable (paper) $10.95

   Beginning Writer's Answer Book, edited by Kirk Polking (paper) $13.95

   Beyond Style: Mastering the Finer Points of Writing, by Gary Provost $15.95

   Discovering the Writer Within, by Bruce Ballenger & Barry Lane $16.95

   Getting the Words Right: How to Revise, Edit and Rewrite, by Theodore A. Rees Cheney $15.95

   A Handbook of Problem Words & Phrases, by Morton S. Freeman $16.95

   How to Increase Your Word Power, by the editors of Reader's Digest $19.95

   How to Write a Book Proposal, by Michael Larsen $10.95

   Just Open a Vein, edited by William Brohaugh $15.95

   Knowing Where to Look: The Ultimate Guide to Research, by Lois Horowitz (paper) $15.95

   Make Every Word Count, by Gary Provost (paper) $9.95

   On Being a Writer, edited by Bill Strickland $19.95

   Pinckert's Practical Grammar, by Robert C. Pinckert $14.95

   The Story Behind the Word, by Morton S. Freeman (paper) $9.95

   12 Keys to Writing Books that Sell, by Kathleen Krull (paper) $12.95

   The 29 Most Common Writing Mistakes & How to Avoid Them, by Judy Delton $9.95

   Word Processing Secrets for Writers, by Michael A. Banks & Ansen Dibell (paper) $14.95

   Writer's Block & How to Use It, by Victoria Nelson $14.95

   The Writer's Digest Guide to Manuscript Formats, by Buchman & Groves $16.95

   Writer's Encyclopedia, edited by Kirk Polking (paper) $16.95

Nonfiction Writing

   Basic Magazine Writing, by Barbara Kevles $16.95

   How to Sell Every Magazine Article You Write, by Lisa Collier Cool (paper) $11.95

   The Writer's Digest Handbook of Magazine Article Writing, edited by Jean M. Fredette $15.95

   Writing Creative Nonfiction, by Theodore A. Rees Cheney $15.95

   Writing Nonfiction that Sells, by Samm Sinclair Baker $14.95

Fiction Writing

   The Art & Craft of Novel Writing, by Oakley Hall $16.95

   Best Stories from New Writers, edited by Linda Sanders $16.95

   Characters & Viewpoint, by Orson Scott Card $13.95

   Creating Short Fiction, by Damon Knight (paper) $9.95

   Dare to Be a Great Writer: 329 Keys to Powerful Fiction, by Leonard Bishop $15.95

   Dialogue, by Lewis Turco $12.95

   Fiction is Folks: How to Create Unforgettable Characters, by Robert Newton Peck (paper) $8.95

   Handbook of Short Story Writing: Vol. I, by Dickson and Smythe (paper) $9.95

   Handbook of Short Story Writing: Vol. II, edited by Jean M. Fredette $15.95

   One Great Way to Write Short Stories, by Ben Nyberg $14.95

   Plot, by Ansen Dibell $13.95

   Revision, by Kit Reed $13.95

Spider Spin Me a Web: Lawrence Block on Writing Fiction, by Lawrence Block $16.95

Storycrafting, by Paul Darcy Boles (paper) $10.95

Writing the Novel: From Plot to Print, by Lawrence Block (paper) $9.95

Special Interest Writing Books

The Children's Picture Book: How to Write It, How to Sell It, by Ellen E.M. Roberts (paper) $16.95

Comedy Writing Secrets, by Melvin Helitzer $18.95

The Complete Book of Scriptwriting, by J. Michael Straczynski (paper) $11.95

The Craft of Lyric Writing, by Sheila Davis $18.95

Editing Your Newsletter, by Mark Beach (paper) $18.50

Families Writing, by Peter Stillman $15.95

Guide to Greeting Card Writing, edited by Larry Sandman (paper) $9.95

How to Write a Play, by Raymond Hull (paper) $12.95

How to Write Action/Adventure Novels, by Michael Newton $13.95

How to Write & Sell A Column, by Raskin & Males $10.95

How to Write and Sell Your Personal Experiences, by Lois Duncan (paper) $10.95

How to Write Mysteries, by Shannon OCork $13.95

How to Write Romances, by Phyllis Taylor Pianka $13.95

How to Write Tales of Horror, Fantasy & Science Fiction, edited by J.N. Williamson $15.95

How to Write the Story of Your Life, by Frank P. Thomas (paper) $11.95

How to Write Western Novels, by Matt Braun $13.95

Mystery Writer's Handbook, by The Mystery Writers of America (paper) $10.95

The Poet's Handbook, by Judson Jerome (paper) $10.95

Successful Lyric Writing (workbook), by Sheila Davis (paper) $16.95

Successful Scriptwriting, by Jurgen Wolff & Kerry Cox $18.95

Travel Writer's Handbook, by Louise Zobel (paper) $11.95

TV Scriptwriter's Handbook, by Alfred Brenner (paper) $10.95

Writing for Children & Teenagers, 3rd Edition, by Lee Wyndham & Arnold Madison (paper) $12.95

Writing Short Stories for Young People, by George Edward Stanley $15.95

Writing the Modern Mystery, by Barbara Norville $15.95

Writing to Inspire, edited by William Gentz (paper) $14.95

The Writing Business

A Beginner's Guide to Getting Published, edited by Kirk Polking $11.95

The Complete Guide to Self-Publishing, by Tom & Marilyn Ross (paper) $16.95

How to Sell & Re-Sell Your Writing, by Duane Newcomb $11.95

How to Write with a Collaborator, by Hal Bennett with Michael Larsen $11.95

Is There a Speech Inside You?, by Don Aslett (paper) $9.95

Literary Agents: How to Get & Work with the Right One for You, by Michael Larsen $9.95

Professional Etiquette for Writers, by William Brohaugh $9.95

Time Management for Writers, by Ted Schwarz $10.95

The Writer's Friendly Legal Guide, edited by Kirk Polking $16.95

A Writer's Guide to Contract Negotiations, by Richard Balkin (paper) $11.95

To order directly from the publisher, include $3.00 postage and handling for 1 book and 50¢ for each additional book. Allow 30 days for delivery.

Writer's Digest Books
1507 Dana Avenue, Cincinnati, Ohio 45207
Credit card orders call TOLL-FREE
1-800-289-0963
Prices subject to change without notice.

Write to this same address for information on *Writer's Digest* magazine, Writer's Digest Book Club, Writer's Digest School, and Writer's Digest Criticism Service.